FORTROSE
ACADEMY

HAPPY ANNIVERSARY!

School magazines have made enjoyable reading in the past, but this edition is not a school magazine in the customary sense; neither does it claim to be a History of the school. It is a collection of reviews, memories, opinions, plans and pictures gathered together to mark the school's 100th. year on its present site.

Some discussion has already taken place on the exact date which we should celebrate. Work on the 'new' Fortrose Academy began at the end of May, 1890; the foundation-stone was officially laid at the end of August, 1890. The formal opening did not take place until March 1892, when the pupils and staff arrived in procession to enter their new school.

Whichever date is chosen, History teachers in the school thought it important that the History Department should compile and make available to all those interested, a unit of work on the History of Fortrose Academy during those formative years. This magazine is the result of that opinion — may all readers find something of interest in the pages which follow!

John D. Campbell.
Principal Teacher of History.
March, 1988.

Contents

FORTROSE ACADEMY 1890-1892

THE FOUNDATION STONE IS LAID.

The laying of the Foundation Stone of the new Fortrose Academy was in fact the second notable event on that Saturday afternoon, for, at 2 o'clock, a ceremony had been held granting Mr Fletcher of Rosehaugh, Chairman of the School Board, the freedom of the burgh. A sketch on the "burgess ticket" showed a view of Fortrose, and included the new Academy. After this earlier ceremony, Mr Fletcher had been the guest at a "cake and wine banquet" in the Royal Hotel.

The "Inverness Courier" of September 2nd, 1890, reports:
"At half-past three o'clock a procession, headed by the local band, was formed in front of the Royal Hotel. First came the Provost, Magistrates, and members of the Town Council, and the members of the School Board, who were followed by the general public. The procession proceeded by way of High Street to the site of the Academy. The building, which is to cost upwards of £1800, was commenced on the 30th of May last, and operations are now well advanced. The plans were prepared by Mr Robertson, architect, Inverness. They show a handsome edifice with Tower, and the building will be equipped with all the latest improvements both as regards lighting and ventilation."

The "Inverness Courier" lists the various contractors, a number coming from Inverness, but the following being from Fortrose:
    Mason   : Mr George Down.
    Plumber : Mr Neil Wilson.
    Plasterer : Mr Duncan Arthur.

The "Inverness Courier" continues:
"..... the foundation-stone was laid by Mr Fletcher with the customary formalities. In the cavity of the stone was placed a bottle containing copies of the Inverness Courier, the Northern Chronicle, the Ross-shire Journal, and Highland News, and also several coins of the realm. Mr Fletcher was presented with a hansome silver trowel and mallet, with which he duly declared the stone to be laid. The inscriptions on the trowel and mallet were as follows:-

> "Presented to J. Douglas Fletcher of Rosehaugh on the occasion of his laying the foundation-stone of the Fortrose Academy Public School —30th August, 1890." "

A number of speeches followed, the last being given by Mr Robertson, the architect; the "Inverness Courier" reports that he ended by saying:
"Mr Fletcher was right in saying that a building with which the children would be so much associated should be pleasing to look upon, and should, like their studies, have a progressive, refining and instructive influence over them. (Applause)."

When finished, the new school was described in an article in the "People's Journal" of March 26th. 1892, as being built on a site,
"which commands an excellent view of the Inverness Firth and the historic stretch of country by which it is fringed. The total cost of the new structure has been close on £1900; but here it should be stated that the internal arrangements are of the most complete, effective, and efficient kind; that even the desks and fittings are of such material as not to tempt the eye or the knife of the most mischievous youngster; and that the classrooms are so arranged that the headmaster will have full command of both his assistants and pupils."

The "People's Journal" included this interesting sketch of the new school:

THE NEW ACADEMY AT FORTROSE.

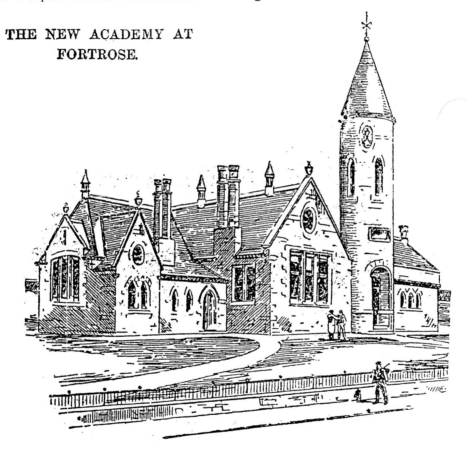

"The Northern Chronicle" of Wednesday, March 9th, 1892, carried this most useful account of the official opening of the new school:

"FORTROSE: OPENING OF NEW ACADEMY.
On Wednesday the new Academy was formally opened by Mr K. Mackenzie, Courthill, Rosemarkie, in absence of the chairman of the School Board, Mr Fletcher of Rosehaugh. The other members of the Board were also present, and a number of the inhabitants. There was nothing in the way of ceremony or demonstration, with the exception that the pupils marched

5

from the old building to the new, and that several gentlemen made short speeches congratulating the Board, teachers and pupils on the favourable change. The old Academy has had an honourable career and many worthy scholars received the elements of their education within its walls, but it has been for some time far too small for its purpose, and it was absolutely necessary to erect a new building. The site chosen is one of the finest in the country. It overlooks the Inverness and Moray Firths, while the building, besides very convenient to the town, is also an ornament to its architecture. There are four school rooms, with nice lavatories, and cloak rooms, and the school furniture is of the very best description. The rooms are all lofty and well ventilated, while the lighting is all that could be desired. A clock ornaments the tower, and was the gift of Mr Fletcher of Rosehaugh. The architect is Mr Robertson, Inverness, who was highly complimented on the comforts, convenience, and general excellence of the new Academy. Short addresses were given by Provost Grant, Revs. C. Falconer, W. Green and J. Macdowal, Mr Henderson, town clerk, and the rector, Mr Laverie, the latter giving some interesting details of the old school during the 14 years he has been in charge."

Mr Laverie,
Rector of Fortrose Academy.
He retired in November, 1913.

Below:
This is a photograph of a picture presented to Rector Mr MacPhail, shortly before he retired in 1972. It was drawn by Erwin Graizer, then a pupil in the school. It shows the original school buildings on our present site.

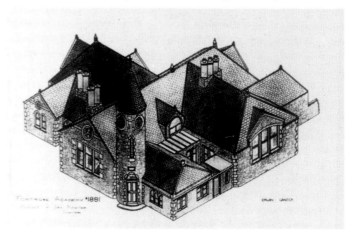

6

This plan shows the layout of the school in 1892.

MORE SPACE PLEASE!
THE SCHOOL BUILDINGS....CHANGES TO 1914

Clearly there was great enthusiasm for the new Fortrose Academy, and certainly few could doubt, either in the 1890s or the 1980s, that good accommodation is a basic necessity for the provision of education. It soon became apparent, however, that the new Academy was short of space. A letter of 29th May 1896, from architect John Robertson to John Henderson, the Clerk to the Academy Board, Fortrose, explains how he (the architect) examined the old academy building with a view to making it suitable for the accommodation of infants. He estimated the cost of the work would be around £98, and he provided details of what was necessary. He also enclosed a sketch for the extension of the Infants Room in the new Academy; this would cost, he estimated, about £170. This latter suggestion was taken up, and another classroom was built out towards Deans Road. This was a "proper" stone construction, not a "temporary" affair.

The early 20th century saw several changes and the main additions are now listed. Plans dated 7/7/1902 show the details of a new cookery room and this was certainly erected very shortly afterwards. It was not, however, of traditional stone structure; neither was the "Manual Instruction Room", which was a wooden building, covered with what looked like corrugated iron sheeting. This woodwork room was placed next to the cookery room, and was ready for use around 1905. The photograph on page 12 shows this room in the background; it can easily be recognised by the style of its windows. Some contributors remember these rooms as two parts of the same building, and this may well have been the case.

An addition which was of more permanent stone was the new science room, probably built just before the "Manual Instruction Room". Certainly plans dated 1904/05 show it already in existence. The photograph (dated "circa 1904") shows the science room clearly; it is easily recognised at the end of the building with its line of windows in the roof. A new main front entrance was also included. (This new science room covered the area where the stage is in the present building.)

Around 1914 another "temporary" building containing two classrooms appeared. These are the rooms described as "Proposed new elementary classrooms" on the 1914 plan. They are also the rooms to become famous (or notorious!) over the decades, for they were to last 50 years, being demolished only to make way for the major extensions of the mid 1960s.

Thus the original buildings which the pupils had entered in March, 1892, had changed considerably by 1914. The pressure on buildings, however, still remained. It seems clear, for instance, that the woodwork room was, before long, to be used as a standard class room, the tools for some time being stored at one end of the room. Equally the room "converted into gymnasium" as the plan says, does not seem for long to have been used for this purpose.

Details of the building are more clearly seen in this picture, taken, possibly, around 1930.

This photograph shows the position of the school's main entrance up to the mid-sixties — at the corner of Deans Road and Academy Street. It also shows much of the accommodation (at right angles to what is now the school kitchen, and called infants classrooms in the plan shown) which was demolished in the mid-sixties.

The view in 1987.
The entrance shown here is for access to the school kitchens, one of the Technical Education blocks and car parking space.

9

FORTROSE ACADEMY

(This plan is dated 1914.)

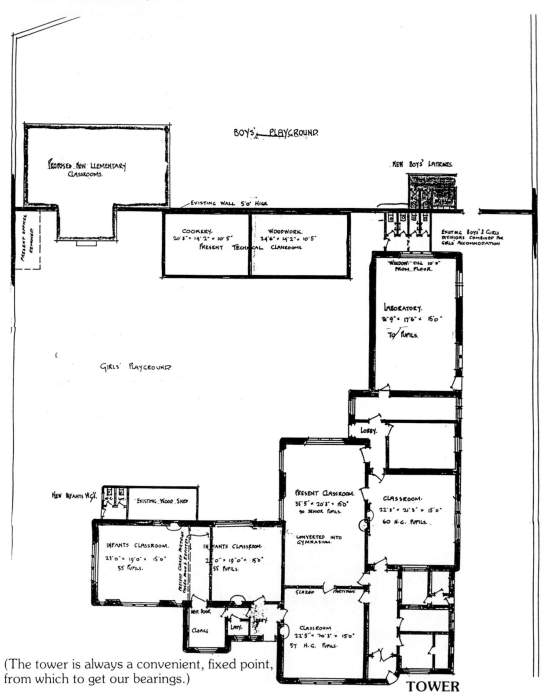

BOYS' PLAYGROUND.

PROPOSED NEW ELEMENTARY CLASSROOMS.

NEW BOYS' LATRINES.

EXISTING WALL 5'0" HIGH

PRESENT OFFICES REMOVED

COOKERY.
20'3" × 14'2" × 10'5"
PRESENT TECHNICAL CLASSROOMS

WOODWORK.
24'6" × 4'2" × 10'5"

EXISTING BOYS' & GIRLS DIVISIONS COMBINED FOR GIRLS' ACCOMMODATION

WINDOW SILL 10'0" FROM FLOOR.

LABORATORY.
31'9" × 17'6" × 15'0"
70 PUPILS.

GIRLS' PLAYGROUND

LOBBY.

NEW INFANTS W.C.

EXISTING WOOD SHED

PRESENT CLASSROOM.
35'5" × 20'3" × 15'0"
90 SENIOR PUPILS.

CLASSROOM.
22'3" × 21'3" × 15'0"
60 H.G. PUPILS.

INFANTS CLASSROOM.
23'0" × 19'0" × 15'0"
55 PUPILS.

INFANTS CLASSROOM.
23'0" × 19'0" × 15'0"
55 PUPILS.

PRESENT CLOAKS METHOD FINISH HOOK & REGISTER

CONVERTED INTO GYMNASIUM.

NEW DOOR

CLOAKS

LAVY.

GLAZED PARTITION.

CLASSROOM.
22'5" × 20'3" × 15'0"
57 H.G. PUPILS.

(The tower is always a convenient, fixed point, from which to get our bearings.)

TOWER

10

THE RECTOR'S LOG BOOK

The school log book records those events which, in the view of the Rector, are sufficiently important to justify a place in the history of the school. Many matters are covered, and the following categories are only a few examples of the kinds of items included: staff lists for each session; changes in the organisation or curriculum of the school; alterations to the buildings or the grounds; visits to, and reports on, the school; absence or illness of a teacher; the reasons for closure of the school; attendance; major changes from the usual routine of the school.

It might at first be thought that the Rector's Log Book would hold little of interest except for those concerned with school affairs. In fact, it can give valuable insights into life in the Black Isle, and the problems of a particular time. Where a detailed log has been written, the reader can study a most precious original source in which there is a vast amount of local detail. The school log books are confidential of course, but permission has been granted to use a number of extracts, and they appear in this magazine under different headings.

Finally, it must be said that in recent years no log book has been kept — apparently there is now no longer any requirement for a Rector to keep such a record.

EXTRACTS FROM THE RECTOR'S LOG BOOK
Days out of school: 1900 - 1924

23 Feb. 1900 : A great many boys absent to-day, having gone over to Fort George to see the Local Volunteers depart for South Africa.

25 May 1900 : Yesterday afternoon was given as a half-holiday in honour of the Queen's birthday.

28 Jan. 1901 : Opened school today after being closed for 5 weeks on account of Christmas holidays and Measles. A medical certificate closed the school from Monday 31st Dec. to the 28th January on account of measles.

17 Oct. 1901 : The Reserve Fleet is today open to the public in Cromarty Firth. A great many boys absent in consequence.

14 April 1904 : Dr Bruce, as president of the Ross-shire Field Club, asked the school board to give a holiday to the schools tomorrow to enable the teachers to view an exhibition of Geological, Botanical and Antiquarian specimens.... In consequence the school will be closed tomorrow.

28 April 1904 : It has been arranged that the Academy scholars are to form a guard at the Episcopal Church door at Miss Hope's marriage, and that the afternoon will be a holiday in honour of the event.

4 Nov. 1904 : Yesterday the school was closed as it was observed as Thanksgiving Day for the harvest.

12 July 1907 : Attendance affected yesterday by the presence of the Channel Fleet in the Bay.

1 June 1917 : Both Miss Kemp and Miss MacAndrew have taken advantage of the summer weather to arrange for an afternoon botanical ramble along the shore accompanied by their classes: the number of specimens culled would alone justify this occasional departure from the regular timetable.

11

6 July 1917	:	Excellent weather continues with excellent benefits. Today Misses Kemp and MacAndrew, with permission, organised a nature ramble in Fairy Glen, & the enthusiasm of their pupils for observation and instruction amply repays the inroad into the ordinary routine of school.
30 May 1919	:	The weather continues dry and sunny. For the whole of the month of May the rainfall has been practically nil. The nights have been cool and dewy, and vegetation has not suffered from the drought. All Departments of the school are encouraged to take advantage of the season to add to their first hand knowledge of nature. Weekly rambles and botanical excursions are highly enjoyed.
19 May 1922	:	The whooping cough is spreading, and the attendance of the Elementary Dept. is down to 75%. The M.O.H. Dr MacLean has given instructions to close the Elementary Dept. for a fortnight, and this has accordingly been done.
16 June 1922	:	Attendance in the HG Dept. fell to 88% owing to a considerable number of pupils having been granted leave of absence on Thursday and Friday to attend a Musical Festival held in Inverness for which they had entered as competitors. The HG School Choir also competed under Miss Mackenzie.
7 March 1924	:	A snowstorm of unusual severity last week-end rendered roads impassible to wheeled traffic. Cromarty and Resolis chidren have not been able to attend school throughout the week, and also some of the pupils from Killen district. Munlochy children have been coming in by train at 11am.

The 1920's.
Back row, left to right: *Major Bain; Charlie Cameron; Donnie Macdonald; Patty Cameron; Albert Hay; Fred Fraser; Ian Macleod; Noel Macgregor; ..... Mackenzie;* Middle row: *Peggy Wilson; Caldie Mann; Bella Williamson; Betty Gordon; Mary Fraser; Margaret Mackenzie; Amy Forbes; Nellie Hay; Annie Macrae; Dorothy Phillips; Hannah Mackenzie.* Front row: *Donnie Mackenzie; Kenneth Grigor; ....; Sandy Young; Allan Macleod.*

THE FIRST WORLD WAR

Memorials to those who died in the First and Second World Wars inform us silently of the tragic loss of life during those years. A study of the war memorials in this area reveals the extent of that loss in the communities of the Black Isle; even for those who perhaps know little of those years of war, it requires no imagination to realise that the many names inscribed on those memorials testify not only to the bravery of those named, but also to the courage with which so many in the Black Isle would have had to face a future without the relatives and friends whose company they had so highly valued.

That staff and pupils in Fortrose Academy were considerably affected by the Great War is clear from the Rector's Log Book. It would in fact be more accurate to say "School" Log Book when referring to those years, for the Rector was himself away for much of the time on active service. Mr Kenneth Macleod, formerly Headmaster of Ullapool Higher Grade School, had been appointed Rector of Fortrose Academy in 1913, assuming duty here on 24th November of that year. He was at that time only 28 years old. After war broke out, Mr Macleod's duties in the army included service in Flanders, and it was some time before he was able to get back to Fortrose. In May 1916, he left to serve with the Forces again, in areas as far as Mesopotamia and India.

The following extracts from the School Log Book deal with the years 1914-18, and will give some idea of the effects of the First World War on the life of our school.

Michael Patience contemplates one of the Black Isle's War Memorials. The photograph was taken in 1986.

Mr Kenneth Macleod.

13

EXTRACTS FROM THE RECTOR'S LOG BOOK

29 Aug. 1914 : The Rector is handing over today the logbook to Mr Henderson, Clerk to the Board, to be kept by him until such time as he can resume duties. The summer holidays have been extended to the 15th Sept. to enable the Board to make a temporary addition to the staff, necessitated by the Rector's absence with the Territorial Army.

17 May, 1915 : Attendance has fallen off again, especially in the Elementary Department. Two cases of measles in Higher Grade Department. Many children absent on account of brothers and relatives killed in France.

31 May, 1915 : In connection with a Butter Making Class for which the School Board have granted the use of the school the apparatus is now stored in the large classroom which is at present not used for teaching.

13 July, 1915 : Academy dismissed this evening for Summer Vacation. Card Certificates were presented by the Chairman to the pupils instead of Book Prizes, as all the children voluntarily agreed to give up to War Funds the money intended to be invested in books.

17 Sept. 1915 : The Board at a meeting this week arranged for the institution of a soup kitchen in connection with the School. The stove of the Cookery Room is to be utilised for cooking the food, and the pupils are to have the meal served in the empty central room. The janitor's wife is to be in charge.

5 Nov. 1915 : The Soup Kitchen has been abandoned this week.

21 Jan. 1916 : The School Patriotic Concert held on Friday last in Fortrose is to be repeated tonight in Rosemarkie.

16 March 1916 : The Infant Mistress, Miss Mackie, married recently, but as her husband is with the Colours, she continues to teach in the Academy, where her services are highly valued.

21 April 1916 : The Academy closed for the Easter Vacation yesterday at midday. We are still short of staff, but the Board has advertised for a temporary teacher and it is hoped we may have an appointment made next week.

22 May 1916 : The Rector who has been able to be in charge for the current session resumes his military duties today and the school is to be conducted by the remaining members of the staff. Mr A. Thom, the senior male assistant will temporarily exercise general supervision.

26 May 1916 : The Nos. in the Rolls are 65 in the H.G. & 106 in Elemy.

5 Jan. 1917 : School reopened on Wednesday, the 3rd. inst. with a thin attendance. There has been a restriction of railway facilities owing to the war, and the customary morning train arrives too late for school. The changed railway time-table came into operation this week, and the long distance children have been unable to attend with their wonted regularity. A number of them are going into lodgings, and others will endeavour to attend school by foot and cycle.

14

25 May, 1917 : Warmer days and a brighter outlook have put new vigour into the children this week and the weekly average of attendance has risen high in the Elementary Classes. The same holds true of the girls in the Higher School. The decrease amongst the boys is to be attributed to a few boys engaged in potato planting. Leaflets urging economy in foodstuffs were distributed this week among the older pupils.

22 Aug, 1917 : The Teaching Staff of the Academy at present consists as follows:

Rector : Kenneth Macleod, M.A. (On War Service).
Assistant Teachers : Archibald Thom, M.A.
John Falconer, M.A.
Miss Chris. Macleod, M.A.
Miss Isabel A. Noble.
Miss M.J. MacAndrew.
Mrs M. Halley.
Miss Cath. M. Kemp.
Music Teacher : Miss S. MacKenzie.

28 Sept. 1917 : The help of Rev. Mr Macinnes has lightened the strain of staffing though it is regrettable that railway connections do not enable him to commence before 11 o'clock each day.

7 Dec. 1917 : Miss Grant obtained leave of absence on Wednesday afternoon to meet her brother who is on his way to the Front.

18 Jan. 1918 : Miss MacAndrew received permission to attend Demonstration Lessons in War Time Cookery on Friday and Saturday of this week. These classes are held under the auspices of the Food Economy Committees at Inverness.

4 Oct. 1918 : The Junior and Senior Classes and Class 1 H.G. were out on Friday afternoon for a Bramble-picking Excursion with the result that, on that afternoon, and on the following day (Saturday) 40 lbs. of Berries were collected, to be made into jam for our troops.

8 Nov. 1918 : A rumour on Thursday evening that Peace had been proclaimed was afterwards contradicted. Work however on Friday departed from the usual routine. The forenoon was spent in singing of patriotic songs in the School Hall where the whole school assembled. In the afternoon the proceedings took the nature of a School Concert, and tea was provided by the staff.

11 Nov. 1918 : (Monday) Information came to hand that the Armistice had been officially and formally signed by the German delegates. The children attending the Academy accordingly formed a procession throughout the streets and school was dismissed at midday.
(Tuesday) A Church Thanksgiving day has been proclaimed. As a result the School Board arranged that the pupils should attend the Service at 12 o'clock and dismiss for the afternoon.

MISS J. HAY

Miss Hay had already given the History Department a great deal of valuable information concerning the Black Isle Railway and I looked forward to another visit to discuss her memories of the 1920s, when she was a pupil at Fortrose Academy; I was particularly keen to hear her recollections of the members of staff and the subjects which they taught.

Miss Hay arrived in Fortrose in 1920, when her family came across from Inverness; from that time, she was a pupil at Fortrose Academy, staying on to the end of her sixth year, when, in 1928, she left to go to Aberdeen University.

It is the case that some pupils know early on in their school days the direction they would like their careers to take when they leave school; I have heard some teachers at Fortrose Academy say that they decided early on that teaching was to be the career for them! Perhaps few, however, can beat Miss Hay — for she, when only seven, told one of her Primary staff that she was going to be a teacher.

In introducing the conversation which follows, it should be made clear that no cassette-recorder was used, and that my notes were the basis for the reconstruction of our conversation.

Miss Hay, when talking to people about their schooldays, I usually find that teachers feature largely in their memories. Is this so in your case?

I was extremely lucky in having the teachers I did, and remember them clearly. Miss MacAndrew, who taught Primaries 6 and 7, was one of my teachers and a very efficient teacher she was. She had learned her teaching skills as a pupil-teacher and was first rate at getting ideas across. Everyone in her classes will remember Miss MacAndrew! Another well-loved primary teacher was Miss Souter; she did not teach me, but taught other members of my family.

My own memories of my Primary teachers are very clear, but I'm afraid I cannot remember much about a number of the teachers I had in the first two or three years of secondary school.

I can certainly remember Miss Isabel Noble, who started me off in Latin; she taught Latin and English to the first and second years pupils — a very inspired teacher! One of her responsibilities was to look after the 'library' — which was a small cupboard let into the wall! Possibly the greatest influence on me was Miss Bowie.... a quiet, intellectual woman and a wonderful teacher. She taught English and History right up through the school.

Can you remember exactly where in the school you were taught by these ladies in your early secondary days?

In the 'Tin Temple'.

What was that? I've never heard of it!

That was the extra building which had been put up on the ground between the main school and Deans Road.

Ah yes.... it had been built in 1914 and lasted until the new buildings were put up in the mid 1960s. I didn't realise it was called by that name.

That 'Tin Temple' was very cold in winter and very hot in the summer. It had two classrooms. Miss MacAndrew was in one of the rooms with her two classes, and Miss Bowie taught in the other room. Miss MacAndrew's room had reasonable desks, but Miss Bowie's room had long benches with metal frames on which the seats were attached — not ideal by any means. Both rooms were small! There was a stove in each classroom. There were no school lunches in those days and pupils, if they wished, could bring in soup and heat it up on the stoves.

I don't think pupils would take too kindly to that in the 1980s!

Later on, the 'Tin Temple' became a Domestic Science room. Both Miss MacAndrew and Miss Noble helped with Domestic Science. Cookery books were issued to the class, and these books had to be covered with canvas or similar material, and then embroidered. No pupil was allowed to use the book until this had been done.

Much more time-consuming than simply covering a textbook with a colourful pop poster as pupils often do now, Miss Hay!

Mr Archibald Thom, who used to live at 1 Castle Street, was the only Science teacher. He taught in a small room, which had a raised area on which stood three washbasins — it was nicknamed the 'Pulpit'. He also taught Geography, but I remember him best for his enthusiastic approach to Botany — he loved the subject and passed on his interest to me. He would arrange lessons, when possible, either at the end of the morning or at the start of the afternoon, so that the lunch hour could be used to add to the time spent rambling. He took us away up the back of Fortrose and along the railway line. I remember being really pleased when I found some 'Scarlet Pimpernel' for it was a plant that was difficult to find in the Black Isle at that time. We would also study the shore, press flowers and plants and find out as much as we could about them. I continued that interest for years afterwards.

Your Rector in the 1920s — that would be Mr Kenneth Macleod?

Yes, 'Mac' of course! That was our nickname for him. We were rather scared of him, but he was certainly a good headmaster, and very efficient. I'll tell you a story about him that I can remember clearly. You know how pupils like to get a teacher away from the work in hand and sidetracked into discussing another 'more interesting' line....

Only too well — some of my senior pupils put their entire effort into getting me off the subject.

One boy in our class, Ernest Burnet, was highly skilled at getting 'Mac' off Latin and on to Scottish History instead, a subject on which the Rector was very keen. One day, when we felt a change from Latin was about due, we signalled Ernest to do his best to ensure some minutes digression. Clearly the Rector must have been aware of what was going on, and becoming somewhat tired of Ernest's attempts to divert his attention, for on that day, he walked straight out of the room, and locked the door — with the pupils inside. His daughter was in the class too. Time wore on — but he didn't come back. We couldn't get out, for we were not able to open the windows. He didn't come back until 6.30 p.m. — he had completely forgotten about us all that time!

17

Your teachers were undoubtedly a colourful set....

The Rector and teachers were second to none. The school itself — buildings, space and so on — may have been poor in many ways, but the members of staff were remarkable. We had a marvellous teacher of French too, far in advance of her time — Miss Hepburn. When I went to university I studied English and French.

I can see that you enjoyed your time as a pupil at Fortrose, and clearly academic standards were good.

In my last year there were nine pupils in the sixth year and all went on to university or some other form of full-time education. My time at Fortrose was stimulating, certainly.

Miss Hay, may I ask now about other subjects you were taught at Fortrose?

We took gym in the Territorial Hall — it was very basic. We also played hockey; I enjoyed being in goal. I cannot remember who took our gym classes — probably a visiting teacher. I can remember our music teacher though. She was a Miss Cameron and she used an ancient gramophone. The school was well known for singing and pupils competed in festivals in Inverness. I remember singing duets with Annie Jack, who had a beautiful soprano voice. The Rector's wife trained a Gaelic choir — after school hours.

May I refer back to something you said earlier, when you spoke of "pupil-teachers". I would like to know more about this method of teacher training.

The scheme operated when I was at school in Fortrose. If you were going to be a teacher, then, when you were in the 4th, 5th, and 6th years, you taught a little yourself! The Rector, Mr K. Macleod, would give future teachers — "pupil-teachers" — instruction in pairs — a boy and a girl — usually after school hours. They would start taking classes in the infant room, then go to the junior primary, then up to Miss MacAndrew's classes. When pupils got as far as taking the "qualifying" class, they could then be called on to teach any class if a teacher was off. Pupil teachers might have taken two lessons a week — in pairs, for the idea was that one would criticise the other.

It must have been quite a daunting prospect to be in charge of a class at so early an age!

It made you either keen on teaching or put you off it for life! Certainly it gave people a chance to see what teaching was like. In the last year an inspector came to examine our teaching. Our Leaving Certificate was stamped under Article 39 if we were satisfactory. I remember as a pupil-teacher here, that I once taught with my hands in my pockets — and got into terrible trouble. On another occasion, when I was taking a lesson on "A Midsummer Night's Dream", the Rector came in to listen. It was quite a good idea really, for teachers looked at your preparation, which had to be thorough.

How did you feel as the end of your pupil days here approached?

I can remember at the end of my last year at Fortrose Academy, when the Prize-Giving Ceremony was taking place — I just did not want to leave. Fortrose Academy was a great influence in my life; there were three areas which had a powerful impact on my life, the school being one, the other two being my home and the Church.

Miss Hay left Fortrose Academy in 1928. Her time there had been not only enjoyable, but also, in academic terms, a success, for she was awarded the dux medal for the Primary School and the gold dux medal in 1928 at the end of her secondary education.

At the time of her graduation from Aberdeen University — in the early 1930s — it was extremely difficult to get jobs. A holiday in London, however was to lead to a long, interesting and enjoyable career as a teacher in the south. It was a successful career too, for Miss Hay became Headmistress of Charles Edward Brooke Grammar School for Girls in 1956. She worked tirelessly to secure the construction of new buildings for her pupils and staff. These new buildings were actually completed in 1968 — the last grammar school to be built.

We tend to think of some areas in education as of recent introduction; Miss Hay was however, a member of the first committee in Croydon on Careers Guidance — before the second World War. The L.C.C. (Predecessor of I.L.E.A.) adopted its proposals later on.

Miss Hay returned to Fortrose when she retired in 1970, and had a house built, in a most delightful situation. At first she felt "like a fish out of water" and longed to go back to London; every post delivery brought letters and cards of good wishes from the south. Then, one day in 1971, Mr MacPhail, Rector of Fortrose Academy, came down to ask Miss Hay if she would be willing to take charge of some English classes for some time, since a teacher at the Academy was to be absent because of ill health. Miss Hay agreed to help out and enjoyed being there; in fact, from that time on, she felt, once again, thoroughly at home in Fortrose. From 1972, Miss Hay was a most efficient invigilator during the S.C.E. examinations. No doubt our pupils were relieved to see the administration of their exams undertaken so competently. Miss Hay continued as an invigilator for a number of years, stopping around 1981.

MRS J.M. MACKENZIE

Members of staff who were in Fortrose Academy in the years up to 1973 will have many memories of Mrs Margaret Mackenzie, and probably the first to come to mind will be one of Mrs Mackenzie walking from the bus stop along to the school every morning. There is, of course, nothing unusual about a teacher walking along to school, except that, in Mrs Mackenzie's case, any of her pupils in the area at the time always wanted to accompany her every inch of the way! In fact her "infants" were not satisfied merely with walking along speaking with their teacher; they would be seen holding on tightly to her arms, sleeves, coat — even her case! I can myself remember this scene clearly, with Mrs Mackenzie apparently completely surrounded by her pupils, making sure her young charges were safely guided to their room.

Mrs Mackenzie's connections with Fortrose Academy are extensive, for she is a former pupil, and taught in the school for many years — from 1947 through to 1973. She thus served under the direction of three Rectors — Mr K. Macleod, who had been Rector in her pupil days, Mr W.D. MacPhail and Mr D.W. MacLeod. In fact, as we shall see, 1973 marked not only her retiral but the end of an important chapter in the history of the school.

Driving over to Conon Bridge during the 1987 summer holidays, I realised that I had not seen Mrs Mackenzie since her retiral fourteen years before! I wondered if I would recognise her again after such a period of years — and whether there was any chance at all that she would recognise me. Arriving at 1 Yew Cottages, I found, at the front door, a very large black and white cat enjoying the warmth of that pleasant afternoon, and apparently guarding the entrance. I need have had no fear about recognising Mrs Mackenzie, for it seemed she had not changed at all. I had no need to introduce myself either, for, as soon as she realised I was at the door, she welcomed me by name.

Mrs Mackenzie's association with Fortrose Academy goes back to the early 1920s, when she arrived as a pupil in the "Qualifying" Class. It should be emphasised that the various stages of schooling in the 1920s were not necessarily known by the names in use today. In fact, different terms might well be used by different people at any one time. Mrs Mackenzie herself remembers that in the 1920s, the first two years of schooling were called the First and Second Infants, followed by Standards 1,2,3,4 and 5, this last year often being called the Qualifying Class, because of the tests pupils sat before entrance to Secondary School: she recounts that pupils who wanted to leave school at 14 stayed on in their primary school, their classes being called Advanced Divisions 1 and 2. Pupils passing the Qualifying tests successfully would proceed to the "Higher Grade", as their secondary education was then more commonly called.

The Prospectus of Fortrose Academy for session 1921-22 gives a detailed description of the organisation of the school. The title page and staff list are shown below.

Ross and Cromarty Education Authority.

FORTROSE ACADEMY
SECONDARY SCHOOL

PROSPECTUS
Session ~ 1921-22

Managers.

ROSEMARKIE and AVOCH S. M. COMMITTEE.

ALLAN MACDONALD, Esquire, *Chairman.*
JOHN HENDERSON, *Clerk and Treasurer.*

School Staff

Rector—
KENNETH MACLEOD, M.A.

Assistant Teachers—
Science Master—ARCHIBALD THOM, M.A.
English Mistress—Miss H. J. BOWIE, M.A.
French Mistress—Miss A. D. TAYLOR, M.A.

General Assistant and Teacher of Needlework to Students in Training—
Miss I. A. NOBLE.

Cookery and Needlework Mistress and Teacher of Senior Div.—
Miss M. J. MACANDREW.

Art Mistress and Teacher of Junior Division—
Miss CATHERINE M. KEMP.

Infant Mistress—Miss J. L. SOUTER.

Music Teacher—Miss MACKENZIE.

Attendance Officer—G. TURNBULL.

20

The Primary Department contained four "Divisions" — Infant, Junior, Senior and Supplementary Divisions. The Prospectus describes the Supplementary Division in these terms:

"SUPPLEMENTARY DIVISION. Pupils who have passed the Qualifying Examination, and who do not desire to continue their studies for three years thereafter, are enrolled in the Supplementary Division of the Primary Department. Parents are respectfully advised not to enrol their children in this Division as the future outlook of pupils so trained is educationally unpromising.

The subjects of the curriculum are English, Arithmetic, Commercial Geography, History (including the growth of the Empire and the study of the institution of Government under which we live), Book-Keeping, Practical Geometry, Practical Science (Boys), Woodwork (Boys), Needlework and Cookery (Girls). On the satisfactory completion of this Course the Pupil is awarded a Merit Certificate by the Scotch Education Department."

One of Mrs Mackenzie's reasons for going to Fortrose was to keep her sister company! Not only did Mrs Mackenzie sit the "Qualifying" examination, she took an extra paper in Arithmetic, which she passed, thereby winning a Bursary of £10 a year for three years. As a pupil in the 1920s, she travelled in to school from Cromarty. She remembers some Cromarty boys sometimes cycling to school at Fortrose. There were of course no school buses in those days, although pupils did use the public service bus. This was operated by Mr Neil Fraser and left Cromarty at 7.45 in the morning. Mrs Mackenzie's sister, Elizabeth Morrison, had been the first to take advantage of this bus when she went to start her days as a Fortrose Academy pupil in "Higher Grade I". The main problem for pupils using this bus came at the end of their school day, for the bus left for Fortrose and Cromarty only after meeting the 6 p.m. ferry at North Kessock. Clearly there was no reason for any pupils using this particular bus to rush out of school when the bell went at 4 p.m.! It was at this time that Mrs Mackenzie and her friends might well get out their games equipment and have an hour of hockey practice. She has still a particular interest in that game and not surprisingly either, for she was captain of the school's senior hockey team, shown in the photograph.

Left to right:
Front row: Betty Gordon, Margaret Campbell, Margaret Morrison (now Mrs Mackenzie), Chrissie Ross and Isobel Moir.
Back row: Kathleen Grigor, Jenny Mann, Jessie Mackenzie, Sheila MacDonald, Jessie Cameron and Dahlia Grigor.

21

A number of teachers took the girls for "Drill", "Gym" or Games; it was a Miss Davidson who did a great deal of work with the hockey team shown in the photograph. Coaching sessions were held after 4 p.m. on Tuesdays, and it is quite possible that it was the first Fortrose Academy hockey team to undertake regular hockey matches with other schools. Mrs Mackenzie clearly remembers playing schools like Dingwall Academy and Inverness High School. She also remembers that a room in the school was used for gymnastics — and for dancing, for there was a piano in that particular room, which was also used for teaching Music. One wonders what our present prinicpal teachers of Music and Physical Education would think of having to share an ordinary class room in which to teach their subjects.

Mrs Mackenzie recalls that Sports Days were very enjoyable and that the school had some athletes who were not only very keen but also very good. The Sports were held in the area outside their Science Room; (i.e. the stage today). The hockey pitch ran at right angles to the school, the football area being parallel to the school. (This area today would be covered by the Assembly and Entrance halls, the quadrangle on its east side and the flagpole area to the west).

As a pupil, Mrs Mackenzie was always most grateful for the considerable kindness shown to her and other pupils by the people of this area. It sometimes happened, when, for instance, rehearsals were being held for concerts, that it was not really possible to get back to Cromarty at night, and other parents nearer the school would welcome pupils into their homes for an over-night stay. Mrs Mackenzie in particular remembers staying with the Rector's family, especially one occasion, when the school's French Department was being inspected by a Dr Macleod, who also stayed with the Rector's family: even the presence of a school inspector did not deter the Rector and his family from helping out when pupils needed accommodation.

After leaving school, Mrs Mackenzie went to Aberdeen Training College; this was the building behind "Robert Gordon's", and was to be the north's centre for training teachers for many years to come. She clearly took her work to heart, for, in her final year, she won first place in Teaching Practice and General Methods — gaining an 'A' in each. This being so, she was invited to teach a lesson in the T.C. Demonstration School for Dr J.C. Smith, the Chief Inspector of Schools, in 1931, a considerable honour.

Mrs Mackenzie was given her first teaching position in January 1932, when she arrived to teach at Culbokie Primary School. This was not a permanent appointment — the early 1930s were far from being good times for many — and Mrs Mackenzie taught there only for a few months, stopping on May 17, 1932. (Since coming to live in Conon Bridge in May 1985, Mrs Mackenzie has actually met some of these former pupils she taught at Culbokie in 1932; one she was speaking to recently is now a grandmother).

In January 1933 Mrs Mackenzie began teaching at Inverpolly Primary School, where she spent four years. Her next position was in the Black Isle, for she began work in Munlochy in 1937, staying there for several years and, thanks to various favourable rector's and inspectors' reports, became established as Infant Mistress. Then, in 1947, came the beginning of a long and happy association with Fortrose Academy.

1949 saw the retiral of Mr K. Macleod, Rector; Mrs Mackenzie remembers the senior pupil who made a presentation to him — now a member of staff in the English Department, Miss E. Macleod! Mrs Mackenzie recalls the new Rector clearly, Mr MacPhail, whom she found to be a man who worked hard, expected hard work of others, and who was endowed with a good sense of humour. The young primary pupils enjoyed a visit from Mr MacPhail, and would readily speak to him about the work they were doing in class.

Mrs Mackenzie taught in a number of rooms over the years, and the mid-sixties no doubt saw her looking eagerly forward to the completion of the new buildings and the conversion of the older school, for she was teaching at the time in one of the "huts". Whatever the accommodation at Fortrose, she always enjoyed her pupils' company, without exception, and found the staff very friendly and co-operative. She taught, too, quite a number of other Fortrose teachers' sons and daughters. Ill health in the family found Mrs Mackenzie considering the possibility of resigning in 1972; the new Rector, however, Mr D.W. MacLeod, persuaded her to stay on for one more year.

The end of the session in 1973 saw both Primary and Secondary teachers gathering in the school canteen to pay tribute to Mrs Mackenzie's years of service in the school. Mr MacPhail, who had retired the previous year, was invited back for this special occasion and he spoke in most complimentary terms of her many years of teaching at Fortrose. Mrs Mackenzie was presented with a gold Omega watch and a leather handbag, and the gathering ended with tea and biscuits. It was a memorable event, for not only did it mark Mrs Mackenzie's retiral, but also the imminent end of a Primary Department at Fortrose Academy.

Mrs Mackenzie — photographed during her years at Munlochy Primary School.

Mrs Mackenzie with a class in Fortrose Academy, — clearly around Christmas time! Among the pupils can be recognised David Sutherland, Erwin Graizer, Tommy Anderson, Alan Macrae, Kenneth Reid, Robert Macrae; James Noble and Paul MacDonald. The whole class is shown in the following picture.

Mrs Mackenzie's Infant class, 1961-62. The pupils are, left to right:
BACK ROW: *Francis Scott; John MacArthur; Ian Reid; Paul Brake; Alan Macrae; Robert Macrae (not related); Alastair MacPherson; David Sutherland; Tommy Anderson; James Noble; Brian MacGregor.* **3rd ROW:** *Isobel Cumming; Shona Elder; Roslyn More; Morag MacKay; Evelyn Currie; Roselyn Mackenzie; Lesley Young; Hilary Mackenzie; Alice MacAngus; Isobel MacAngus (Twins); Fiona MacCuish.* **2nd ROW:** *Robert Innes; Francesca MacIntyre; Kathleen Ross; Carol Anderson; Jayne Junor; Kathy Holm; Sheena MacRae; Linda MacKeddie; Donella MacKay; David Bisset.* **FRONT ROW:** *Tommy Kane; Alan Mann; Kenneth Gill; Laurie Chancellor; Johnny Mackenzie; Kenneth Reid; Erwin Graizer; Jimmie Connor; Bruce Morrison; Stephen Beattie; David Mackay.*
(Absent: Jane Anderson.)

MR R. MACRAE

Few pupils beginning their education at Fortrose Academy around 1920, could have imagined that the 1980s would see them back working in the same school. Yet this has happened to Mr Macrae, for he works on Tuesdays and Fridays in the Technical Education Department, concerned not only with the maintenance of the many tools there, but in other general work preparing equipment, steel and wood for use in technical education. He was busily engaged there when I called to ask for an interview. A few days later, absorbed in some earlier plans of the school, I invited Mr Macrae to recall details of his Primary teachers and the rooms in which they taught......

Miss Souter took the first three classes in one of the "infants school rooms" as they are called on your plan. A partition separated our room from Miss Kemp's room next door. Miss Souter's room had about two metres of flat area at the front, then there were rows of desks stepped up towards the back of the room; there was a space behind the back row for pupils to move around.

I didn't realise the room was arranged like that — something like the balcony in a cinema! What are these semi-circles in the rooms?

Heating! The fires were enclosed in stoves with front opening doors and there were cement hearths for safety. You can see the coal storage area marked on the plan; there was another shed — behind the infants' room — which was used for storing anthracite or wood. Mr Thom, who taught Science, used anthracite for the type of fire he had. The janitor lit the fires in the morning, then teachers saw that their fire was kept going. Getting the fuel for the fire was sometimes used as a form of punishment exercise!

After leaving Miss Souter's classes, you went into Miss Kemp's room on the other side of the partition?

That's right. I always remember Miss Kemp teaching us about the mountains of Scotland, for we had to recite — and sing — them clearly. We would chant "Ben Wyvis, Beinn Dearg, Ben Nevis" and so on and always include "Ben Jack" — not a mountain, but one of our pupil's nicknames. I'm afraid he (Sonny Jack) died on his initial army training on the parade ground. After Miss Kemp, Miss MacAndrew took us for the last two years of Primary School. She was a strict disciplinarian; I can remember that some pupils were rather fearful as we waited to go into her room for the first time — but we soon realised that she was very good at imparting knowledge.

Yes, Miss Hay said that she was a first-rate teacher. She taught in the building called the "Tin Temple" — Do you remember calling it by that name? •

I believe I do now that you mention it. Miss MacAndrew took the class just before it went on to the Higher Grade, or Secondary, as you would call it today. She also took cookery for the girls; the cookery room had a big black stove with three rings for cooking. I remember Miss Noble taught in the classroom next to it; it had once been a woodwork room, but woodwork was stopped as the room was needed as an ordinary classroom. The tools, however, were stored for some time at the end of Miss Noble's room! Miss Bowie was a very nice teacher, with good control over her pupils; when pupils entered her room for the first time, she told them she would stand for no noise. She said she had a strap, but added that she hadn't used it and hoped that she wasn't going to start. Pupils were always well behaved in her class. Of course, things were generally fairly strict. You would always salute a teacher if you met one in the street. The Rector would always return your salute.

Yes; Miss Hay told me that, when she was a pupil, she would curtsy when she met a member of staff. Did you live near the school, Mr Macrae?

I lived in Academy Street in the twenties; I went home for my lunch — there were no school lunches then, of course. Cromarty pupils had a long wait for their bus at the end of the day, and the Rector would allow them into his classroom after four to heat up some food to keep them going until they got home.

As you know, a number of our pupils today take on jobs after school, or at weekends and holidays to earn some money. Potato holidays especially can be very useful. Did you do anything like this?

Yes; as far as I remember, we did get potato holidays — probably about a week. There were plenty of small farms very close-by — on the Ness for instance — which have now disappeared. Perhaps about six have now gone. In the summer months, when I was about 12 years old, I spent a large part of my holidays caddying for the guests at the Hawkhill Hotel, which was run at that time by Mrs Kennedy. I would probably do two rounds a day; the rate of pay would vary with the time of year — it might be 1/6 in July, but 2/6 in August. The wealthier guests often came later on in the season. The young caddies supported their players with great enthusiasm. I can remember I always caddied for Dr Stewart, and I certainly remember his pipe! I also caddied for Mr Latta's father — a very pleasant man. We spent the money we earned on clothes and boots, or on things for the home.

I notice that in photographs taken in the early 20th. century, the youngsters here are usually barefooted; would that have been the case when you were around primary school age?

In the summer in our young days, we seldom wore shoes; shoes were always worn to school though.

Did you study any foreign languages in your 'Higher Grade' days?

Miss Noble taught me Latin for the first years in secondary. I was taught French by Miss Hepburn. It came in useful when I was abroad during the war.

I have heard that you took part in the landings in Italy and at Normandy — is that correct?

Yes; I was a tank driver, working with both amphibious and ordinary tanks. At one stage during the North African campaigns we were on the last bridge before Tripoli when I met Tommy Fraser of the Highland Division. He is a former pupil of Fortrose Academy, and I was particularly pleased to see him; shortly before we met, he had got some whisky and cigarettes — but they had been stolen!

We must arrange another meeting to get information about your experiences in the war. Personal accounts and memories often describe details seldom to be found in standard books. Finally, Mr Macrae, I believe you have yet another connection with Fortrose Academy. Is it right that you actually worked on the construction of the new buildings which were put up in the 1960s?

Hall's of Aberdeen did that job, and I was working for them then. The building went up fairly quickly, the new accommodation going up before the old buildings were touched. Artificial stone was used to get as good a match as possible with the natural stone of the old buildings. Joiners were greatly in demand in the mid-sixties. We worked on a bonus system, getting so much for completing certain stages on time.

Mr Macrae, thank you for giving me so much information; I'll use some in interview form and you will recognise other details you have described to me elsewhere!

"...things were generally fairly strict..."

The 1920's.
Back row, left to right: *Miss Kemp; James Mackenzie; Billie McIver; Freddy Wilson; Roddie Fraser; Kenny MacDonald; ....Mac Bain.*
Front row: *Margaret Campbell; Dolly Mackay; Cathie Mackenzie; Alice Allan; L. Civil; Nina MacIver; Maria Watson; Nellie Simpson; Leila Cameron; Janet Maclean; Dahlia Grigor; Jenny Mann.*

The 1920's.
Back row, left to right: *Malcolm Macrae; Dougal Corbet; Alastair Sutherland; George Junor; George Clark; "Bunty" Mackay.*
Third row: *Hugh Macdonald; ....; Alastair Maclean; ...... Matheson; Willie Junor; John Bain; George Cameron; John Watson; George Hossack.* Second row: *Effie Watson; Maisie Fraser; Jean Hay; Jenny Fraser; Kathleen Grigor; Gretessie Mackay; Madge Mackenzie; Lizzie Macdonald; Nina Cameron; Evelyn Mann; Aggie Millar.* Front row: *Ronald Macrae; Alastair Campbell; Campbell Hastie; Kenny Mackenzie; George Cameron; Willie Mackenzie; Willie Mann; Angie Mackeddie.*

The 1920's.

Back row, left to right: .... Arthur Riach; .... R. Macbain; Albert Hay; Ian Munro; .... Kenneth Grigor.
Middle row: Allan Macleod; Sandy Young; Lottie Macdonald; Elsie Macleman; Mary Fraser; Betty Gordon; Louis Patience; ? Mackenzie.
Front row: Peggy Wilson; Hannah Mackenzie; Rhoda Geddes; Isobel Moir; Chrissie Ross; Betty Miller.

30

The 1920's.
From the left: *Mr Fleming; the young girl is "Nornor" Stuart; Gentleman behind her unknown; Mr Macrae; Mr K. Macleod; Mr Fraser; Major Stuart.*

MISS H. YOUNG

Miss Young's address in Fortrose includes the word "Farmhouse", which suggests an interesting link with the past and after arriving at her home, I found this to be the case. Miss Young's parents owned the farm here and this was the home where she had spent her childhood. The farm's outbuildings have now largely disappeared, and new houses have been built in many of the surrounding areas; in a car, passers-by may not be fully aware of the nature of the house, since a gable-end is seen from the road, but for walkers, it will be clear that here is a home of considerable character, with a fascinating history.

Once inside, my attention was attracted by a photograph which gave a delightful view of a binder in action on the Ness in days gone by, with the cliffs and higher areas near Rosemarkie in the background. The binder is being pulled by three horses — three mares in fact, called "Bess", "Norah" and "Poll" — short for Polly. A brother of Miss Young is driving the three horses, another brother is lifting the sheaves and a third helper is also shown. The field is the one situated behind the Golf Clubhouse. I had to remind myself that the purpose of the visit was to secure Miss Young's help in clarifying some details of the History of Fortrose Academy, otherwise the whole evening might well have been spent on these other aspects of local history — hopefully another time!

Miss Young's primary schooldays were spent at Rosemarkie; she actually passed slightly less time than usual in the early infant class, for an elderly lady, to whom she had delivered milk, had taught her to read before going to school. After the "Qualifying" class, she went on to her secondary education — the "Higher Grade" as we have seen it was then called.

At Fortrose Academy, a number of influences played their part in shaping Miss Young's ideas, but probably one of the most important was the impact of Miss Bowie's teaching. Miss Young remembers Miss Bowie as a tall, slim, quietly spoken woman, with an extensive understanding of her subject; discipline in her class was always very good, for she captured the interest of her pupils. Certainly, she gave Miss Young an enduring love of her subject — English.

Miss Young was able to shed light on whether or not accommodation in the school had been reserved for "drill" or "gym", and indeed, she had a particular reason for remembering that it had. On one occasion, Miss Young had been teaching another pupil to dance in the "gym" — at a time when, perhaps between classes, she should have been making greater haste to get to her next teacher — and the Rector arrived on the scene and cleared the two pupils from the room, there being no one else in it at the time. It is therefore certainly the case that a standard classroom was used for gym lessons for at least some time, however brief; with little specialist equipment, lessons were mostly in the nature of exercises. Hockey was popular outside, and Miss Young has good reason to remember that game, for a friend hit her accidentally with a hockey stick, breaking one of her teeth!

Miss Young found the Academy a happy and well disciplined school, with Mr K. Macleod not only an efficient Rector but a good class teacher. Pupils were expected to be well behaved and punctual in arrival at school. Miss Young sometimes ran back to her home at lunchtime; any late return, by the smallest of margins would result in trouble! Her grandmother came to live in Academy Street, thereby providing a much nearer refuge for a hot meal in the winter. She remembers the school day starting at 9am and finishing at 4pm, with the lunch hour from 1-2pm.

Miss Hay had said that everyone at school at that time would remember Miss MacAndrew, a teacher of the classes we would now call Primary 6 and 7. Miss Young attended primary school, as we have seen, at Rosemarkie, but she recalls Miss MacAndrew as the teacher who took the girls for cookery. It is clear that one feature of these earlier days is the fact that each teacher might well be involved in teaching a variety of subjects. For some time, we became accustomed, in secondary education, to the specialist teacher who tackles one particular subject area, although it must be said that this subject specialism has in recent years come under attack. In the 1920s too, and for some decades thereafter, the Rector was extensively involved in class teaching, a role that was in most schools to change in later years. One interesting practice has , in a sense, returned as far as Fortrose pupils are concerned, and that is the involvement of senior pupils in the work of the primary schools. No one is suggesting for one minute that "pupil-teachers" still exist in the earlier sense, but our senior pupils, during session 1987-88, have visited Primary Schools to make themselves known to the pupils who will before long, be arriving at Fortrose Academy. These visits provide a most valuable link between the Academy and its feeder primary schools, let Primary pupils see and get to know the seniors at Fortrose, and give the Fortrose pupils most worthwhile experience in meeting primary staff and pupils. The experiment has proved very popular with the pupils involved, and has a great deal of practical benefit to offer in the way of encouraging yet further communication between the schools in the Black Isle.

Miss Young left Fortrose Academy at the end of her fifth year. Her schooldays there were clearly hardworking, for her name appears a number of times in the prize lists of the 1921/22 school prospectus. She studied at Glasgow University, from which she graduated in 1926. She attended Jordanhill Training College in Glasgow for two years. This extra time at Training College is explained by the fact that there was a new course available, and Miss Young completed this extra course in English. Her first teaching position was at Fortrose Academy —a temporary position, since she was taking Latin classes for Mr K. Macleod, who was absent through illness. Her first permanent appointment came as a teacher of the "qualifying" class at Lochcarron Primary School, a position she was happy to secure, in view of the unemployment difficulties referred to earlier. Unfortunately, ill health proved troublesome over the next few years, and Miss Young left Lochcarron in 1937. Taking a holiday in the south of England, she became involved in tutoring work in Surrey.

1940 saw Miss Young's return to the north, for she arrived to teach English at Tain Royal Academy. She enjoyed her years at Tain, and stayed there until her retirement in 1973 — a considerable period of service in one school. It goes without saying that she enjoyed her visits to Fortrose during her "Tain years", visits which became easier and more frequent after she bought a car in 1957. Miss Young speaks with great affection about the schools in which, as a pupil or as a teacher, she spent many happy years.

MRS M. SINCLAIR

Mrs Sinclair has handed over several photographs which will be most useful in our local history studies. She also provided several class photographs of Fortrose Academy pupils in the 1920's, a number of which are shown. Her interest in local history has been of great value and, with the help of some friends, she very kindly provided the names of the pupils of the twenties.

Mrs Sinclair can remember her late mother telling her about the time she walked with all the other pupils from the old Academy to the new school, in March, 1892! It may be said that today Mr and Mrs Sinclair have very close connections with local education, for they stay in the building that was once Rosemarkie Primary School! The photograph shows Mrs Sinclair at her front door in 1987.

One of the pleasant views from the school (1987).

THE SCHOOL BUILDINGS
1933: RECONSTRUCTION AND EXTENSION

Major alterations and additions in the early 1930s considerably changed the appearance of Fortrose Academy. New accommodation was built out from the science room (the present stage); they are the rooms which now form the Business Studies Department. (They have undergone internal changes since becoming Business Studies' accommodation.) A corridor ran alongside the new rooms — part of the present corridor — and toilets and cloakrooms to replace those demolished, were built at right angles to this new block. It was at this time that the underground boiler house was installed, the school now enjoying coke fired central heating; a Brockhouse Boiler from Manchester was used. A small staff room was situated close by the boiler house — very close in fact, for one present member of staff can remember a teacher often confusing one door with the other!

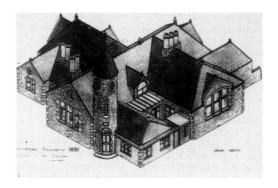

This picture shows how this part of the school changed in the 1930s.

Here is a photograph of the same area in 1987. The roof line and large windows of the older buildings were further altered in later developments.

The other important changes of the 1933 period involved the existing buildings. The area on the south side of the school (from the tower up to the Rector's class room) was completely altered; the Rector's study, boys cloakroom and the open court and coals area disappeared to make way for one large room. We are lucky to have a photograph showing this — although it was taken some years later. A photograph of Mr Graizer's picture is again shown to help appreciate the change.

The Rector's Log Book gives some interesting comments about the changes of the 1930s. Two extracts are given below:

"14th APRIL, 1933.
The alterations and extensions of the school are now in hand, and the main building has been vacated. The Primary Dept. are accommodated in the Ex-Servicemen's Hall and the Church of Scotland, the senior division under Miss McAndrew being housed in the latter. These halls are furnished with school desks etc. removed from the Academy.

Class I and II of the Secondary Dept. are accommodated in the new Town Hall which has been similarly furnished from the Academy. Class III is in the St. Andrews Church Hall and Classes IV and V in the Spiers building in the Academy grounds hitherto used as classrooms. The Town Hall has no fireplace but otherwise it is suitable, lavatories having been under construction during the work. A lavatory is also being constructed at the Ex-Servicemen's Hall."

"2nd SEPT, 1933.
The Academy reopened on Tuesday the 29th August, in the reconstructed and extended buildings. Workmen are still busy completing their work, but except for the woodwork and cookery classes there is no difficulty in finding accommodation for the work of the school. 52 new single desks have been supplied, and the remaining desks, all dual, have been repaired where it was necessary, stained and varnished. All the other furniture of the school has been similarly treated, and the schoolrooms are commodious, well lit and ventilated. Fireplaces have been done away with and a system of central heating installed. The school is also lit with electricity, and the school yard has been gravelled."

(The temporary classrooms marked on the 1914 plan as "Cookery" and "Woodwork" were demolished at this time.)

THE RE-OPENING CEREMONY

The "Ross-shire Journal" of 8th September, 1933, gave an excellent account of the re-opening of the reconstructed building. The management of the Ross-shire Journal Ltd. has kindly granted its permission for the use of a number of articles in this magazine; a number of most informative extracts are now quoted.

> "The re-constructed Fortrose Academy was formally opened on Tuesday, the ceremony being performed by Sir Robert Brooke of Midfearn, Bart., Convener of the County Council of Ross and Cromarty, in presence of a large and enthusiastic gathering of people, representative of the town and district. The function took place in front of the Academy in delightful weather. The pupils paraded at the front door of the Academy, while the general public gathered in a circle round the pupils."

Provost Rolling gave a brief outline of the history of the Academy. He commented on the possible reasons for the selection of Fortrose as an educational centre:

"Fortrose, it appeared, was chosen as an education centre on account of its amenities, fine air, sea bathing and its few distractions from study and equally few temptations. These conditions still existed."

The Provost introduced Sir Robert Brooke, who said that he was glad that the additions to the buildings had at last been built. He referred to the serious depression of the period and said that people could not expect the same rate of progress that had been maintained in years of prosperity. He spoke of the criticisms directed against those in the County Council. The "Ross-shire Journal" continues:

"Mr D. Matheson, architect, then presented Sir Robert Brooke with a solid gold key, inscribed as follows:
'This key was presented by the architect and contractors to Sir Robert Brooke of Midfearn, Bart., County Convener of Ross and Cromarty, when he officially re-opened the re-constructed Fortrose Academy — 5th September, 1933.'"

The Rector, Mr Kenneth Macleod, spoke in praise of those people who had fought to secure new buildings at Fortrose. He pointed out that a school should be judged by its achievement, not by its size. He paid a particular tribute to architect Mr Matheson, and to Provost Rolling. Mr F.W. Michie, the Chief Inspector of the Highland Division, also addressed the gathering. A half-holiday was granted to the pupils, and at the end of the ceremony those present took the opportunity to inspect the new buildings.

The "Ross-shire Journal" describes the buildings:

"The additions to the Academy consist of three new classrooms, boys and girls cloakrooms, lavatories and staffrooms. Classrooms and cloakrooms are connected by covered ways. All the old classrooms have been remodelled, windows being enlarged and cross ventilation introduced, making them bright and healthy.

A particularly happy and pleasing feature is the decoration of the infants' room with sea and landscapes as well as animal life such as appeal to the little ones.

Externally the new classrooms have been built upon pleasing but economical lines and blend well with the older parts of the building, which are of rather elaborate appearance and which were constructed in better times and when building costs were a mere fraction of what they are today."

The 1933 extension (or most of it — 2 of its 12 windows are not included) is shown to the left of the picture. The later additions of the 1950s (lighter in colour) stand out clearly in this photograph taken shortly after the completion of the 1950s additions.

1950's ADDITIONS

A brief description may be here included on the accommodation which made its appearance around the 1950s. The most notable development of the early fifties was the addition to the block built in the 1930s. (Shown in the previous picture.) The 1950s buildings contained rooms for Domestic Science and Technical Subjects. The chimney nearer the camera was for the large Aga cooker in the Domestic Science Department, the chimney at the end of the building being for the forge used in metalwork.

By this time — the mid-fifties — the lay-out of the school must have presented a somewhat long and narrow appearance. Certainly the views from the rooms facing the south must have been very pleasant, with grass just outside and no doubt farming scenes close-by, distracting the attention of the pupils!

Such then were the main buildings of Fortrose Academy by the 1950s. They were to stay virtually unchanged in external appearance at any rate, until the mid-sixties. The description of the buildings to this point is not yet quite complete, for a brief mention must be made of the "temporary" forms of accommodation which made their appearance over those years.

This picture, taken around 1955, shows the school canteen. The kitchens ran parallel to the main school buildings, which are also to be seen in the photograph. The dining-hall was at right angles to them. The dining-hall door is clearly visible, and beyond can be seen the girls' toilets and covered shelter.

Another "hut" was installed at the end of the canteen kitchens; yet another "hut" was put up at the east end of the school (ie. at the end of the 1950s extension). This last affair did not last long for all the temporary accommodation — including the famous "Tin Temple" which had lasted so long — was demolished when the new school buildings went up in the mid-sixties!

This picture shows the additions of the 1930s and 1950s as they appeared in 1987. They had been reharled in the mid-sixties; the large door, at the end near the camera, appeared in the early 1970s.

"IN THE PICTURE...."
(some memories of the 1930's)

School outings are frequent occurrences in the 1980's, and pupils are given several opportunities to journey far and wide in this country and abroad. Conditions in the earlier part of this century were such that it would be quite unrealistic then to expect anything like the possibilities for pupil travel that exist today. Nevertheless, those chances which were given were eagerly grasped and thoroughly enjoyed. Both Messrs. A and D Sutherland remember a trip to Nairn in the mid-twenties, when virtually the whole secondary department boarded the "Ailsa" (the boat normally plying between Cromarty and Invergordon, and owned by Mr Watson) and set off across the Firth. A group of pupils provided musical entertainment on board, and on arrival at Nairn, further amusement was supplied by the "Pierrots" — travelling entertainers performing their singing and juggling acts in the open air.

We are very fortunate in having some photographs of a school outing in the mid-thirties, when a school picnic was arranged near the Black Rock area. The photographs were donated by Mrs H. Wilson, a daughter of Mr K. Macleod, Rector from 1913 to 1949. Mrs Wilson remembers the thirties well, for she was a pupil in Fortrose Academy at the time. (A check on the records shows that in 1936 Hazel Macleod (i.e. Mrs Wilson) was awarded the Laverie Prize in Mathematics, the award consisting of a "gold wristlet watch"). Mrs Wilson recalls that it was in the early 1930's that her father bought his first car — a Renault. It was purchased in Inverness and his driving instruction consisted of a run to Dores and back! He had used motorised transport before the acquisition of the Renault, for he had previously owned a motor cycle and sidecar. Mrs Wilson explains that the family had some exciting times in their first car, for Mr K. Macleod did not manage completely to master the art of driving!

A most interesting picture! It shows, from left to right:
Miss MacAndrew; Miss Noble; Miss Kemp; Miss Mackenzie; Miss Bowie; Miss Hepburn.

It is sad to record that Miss Mackenzie became ill in March, 1937 and died the following month. On the day of her funeral, the school was closed and "the Rector accompanied by all the male members of the staff attended the funeral at Fodderty." (Rector's Log Book.) Miss Mackenzie had been a very popular teacher and her pupils wanted to do something to honour her memory. The picture shown on page 40 was bought for this purpose.

The picture "A Boy with a Rabbit" is to be seen in the school canteen.

This picture shows a pipe-smoking Mr Matheson and Rector, Mr K. Macleod.

Here are four pupils enjoying the cool of the river at that school picnic. They are, from the left: Peggy Craig; Ellen Black; Hazel Macleod; Elsie Ross.

This mid-1930's picture shows Mr K. Macleod in procession with senior pupils in the High Street. Christine Craig (Mrs MacQueen) is on the Rector's left. The occasion was King George V's Silver Jubilee or possibly the coronation of King George VI.

Mrs Wilson photographed outside her home in 1987. She returned to Fortrose Academy to teach in the Home Economics Department from 1974 - 78.

THE SECOND WORLD WAR

The school's memorial tablet.

Listeners to the Prime Minister's wireless broadcast of 3rd September 1939 must have been overwhelmed by a sense of tragedy; their worst fears had come true; European war was yet again to tear their lives apart. 3rd September 1939 was a Sunday, and the time of the broadcast 11.15am. No doubt many were about to go to church when the news came; certainly those already on their way would hear the news from their minister and would return home early.

Many people in 1939 would have been old enough to remember the Great War of 1914-18, and the millions of deaths and casualties it had caused. There seemed every reason in 1939 to believe that this new war would be even more horrific, bringing devastation to vast areas of Britain itself.

There had been civilian casualties in Britain during the First World War. The developments in aircraft capabilities since that time, and the belief that little could be done to stop bombers reaching their targets, now meant that, in 1939, many expected millions of deaths in Britain as a result of bombing. Gas attacks too were greatly feared and indeed millions of gas masks had been issued by 1938.

To our pupils today, these fears may seem very distant for many of the once obvious effects on our school and communities, brought by the war, have disappeared. There are, for instance, to the casual visitor's eye, few signs of the many airfields that were to be seen during the war years in this area of Scotland.

Clearly this area was deeply affected in a variety of ways during those years of war. The Rector's Log Book gives a most fascinating account of the effects of the war on the life of those in Fortrose Academy. Some of Mr K. Macleod's entries are now included.

EXTRACTS FROM
THE RECTOR'S LOG BOOK

1 Sept. 1939   : On account of the Government evacuation plans for certain cities and towns, the buses were withdrawn today from the local service and the Academy was closed at 1pm to enable children to walk home. Some have to go long distances.
The staff was engaged on plans connected with the billeting of evacuees all afternoon. War has not yet been declared, but everything points to an ultimatum by Parliament tonight.

15 Sept. 1939 : School resumed on Monday with a very good attendance. The Secondary Roll is now 114 and the Primary 93, the former being the highest recorded since the institution of the Secondary Dept. Some of the fresh enrolments are due to the influx of children from the south in consequence of the fear of bombing of cities by the Germans. With the hearty support of Fortrose parents trenches of a sheltering type have been dug in the school playground. The Convener of the County, Major Stirling of Fairbairn, inspected them yesterday, and Dr Middleton, Chairman of the local School Management Committee, today. H.M.I. Mr Gunn visited the school on Tuesday to make a preliminary survey of available school accommodation in case of forcible evacuation of children from the south.

29 Sept. 1939 : Two afternoons have been devoted to revetment of trenches. A good deal of work still remains to be done. Only the boys of the 2 senior classes are engaged in this work.

13 Oct. 1939   : The ARP trenches have today been virtually completely revetted and sandbagged, and the whole school including the staff were comfortably accommodated in them for practice purposes today.

17 Nov. 1939 : The Shelter Trenches were inspected on Thursday by the Officer in charge of such work for the County, and verbally highly commended.

24 Nov. 1939 : Library Service on account of the Blackout is to be carried on for the next two months on Saturdays at 2pm.

8 Dec. 1939   : Gas masks need not for the present be carried to school by pupils or teachers, according to a circular issued by the Director of Education.
A nominal roll of all children attending school who were voluntarily evacuated from other districts on account of the war was forwarded to the Education Office yesterday. The total number was 18 of whom 11 are still in attendance.

10 May 1940 : In view of the invasion of the Low Countries today by the Germans, certain repairs were made to the shelter trenches by the senior boys. Instructions were given for Gasmasks to be on view for inspection on Monday morning at the school.

17 May 1940	: Miss Munro, teacher of Domestic Science, conducted a demonstration in War Time Cookery to local housekeepers on Wednesday in the Cookery room from 3 to 4pm. There were 17 ladies present together with the senior girls of the Secondary Dept. As from last Monday pupils have carried their gas-masks with them to and from school.
10 June 1940	: A war Savings Group has been formed in the school.
4 July 1940	: The County Council suspended expenditure on prizes on account of the war, and accordingly only prizes and medals presented by friends of the school were awarded.
30 Aug. 1940	: During the vacation there was a cloudburst in the Cromarty District and the road via Newhall is still closed. Consequently, pupils from that district have been unable to attend this week. The heavy rain in Fortrose during the day of the cloudburst had the effect of destroying a side of one of the shelter trenches in the playground. The weight of water and sandbags caused some of the uprights to break and the revetting timbers gave way in a number of places. The remaining trenches stood up to the strain and are intact.
29 Nov. 1940	: The Academy opened this week at 9.20 instead of 9am on account of the Blackout regulations and the retention of the summer time arrangements in the country.
14 Feb. 1941	: The Rector was absent on Tuesday afternoon attending a meeting of the sponsors of the Air Training Cadet Corps for Ross-shire.
21 Feb. 1941	: For the first time since war was declared an alert was sounded on Wednesday at 1.45, during the dinner interval. The staff made their way quickly to the school to take whatever appeared to be the most advisable steps for the protection of the pupils.
28 Feb. 1941	: An A.T. Corps in connection with the Ross-shire mainland unit was formed in the Academy today.
10 March 1941	: 3 stirrup pumps and 6 pails for firefighting were delivered at the school today by the Officer in charge of Fire Prevention for the County.
23 March 1942	: The Film van of the Ministry of Information visited the school on Tuesday and two performances of an hour each were given in the Music Room.
17 April 1942	: Two elaborately constructed shelters against bombing have been erected close to the school, and the keys handed to the janitor.
8 Jan. 1943	: A school canteen was opened on Tuesday and a hot meal of 2 courses served to the Primary Dept. as from 12.30, and to the Secondary Dept. from 1 o'clock. Woodwork instruction has been meantime abandoned for lack of accommodation, and agriculture is to be substituted.
11 June 1943	: In connection with the Wings for Victory week held in the Burgh, the School gave a concert in the Town Hall last night, and owing to the unsatisfied demand of the public has to be repeated tonight as the accommodation of the Town Hall is too limited. All seats were sold last night at reserve prices.

6 Aug 1943	:	The Academy reopened on Tuesday the 3rd August. The roll is 213 of which 95 are in the Secondary Dept. 140 pupils have this week been partaking daily of the dinners provided in the School Kitchen, and an application for permits to buy increased rations has been sent to the Food Office.
3 Sept. 1943	:	On this the 4th anniversary of the Declaration of war, Rev. Wm. Craig B.D., Fortrose, held a religious service at the school main gate, which was attended by all the pupils and teachers present.
9 June 1944	:	Major Grant, an officer on the staff of the War Office, visited the school this afternoon and gave a most informative address to the Secondary boys on parachuting and gliding.
11 May 1945	:	Tuesday and Wednesday of this week were observed as National Holidays in celebration of the unconditional surrender of Germany to the Allies. The school was accordingly closed.
17 Aug. 1945	:	This has been an eventful week. The Prime Minister in a midnight broadcast on Tuesday announced the end of the Japanese war and the surrender of the Japanese Empire to the Allied powers. He also proclaimed a public holiday for the 2 days following. School was accordingly closed on Wednesday and Thursday, and in the afternoon of the latter day all children in the Burgh and Parish were entertained to tea, games, singing and dancing in the Town Hall by the Town Council acting on behalf of the citizens. A souvenir gift of a newly-minted florin was also made to each child.

THE SCHOOL'S MEMORIAL TABLET

The entry of June 1, 1949 in the Rector's Log Book records:

"The staff of the school, having decided that a memorial tablet should be erected in memory of former pupils who gave their lives in the two World Wars, raised a fund for this purpose from themselves, some former teachers and former pupils. There was a very hearty response from the former pupils who were circularised, and now the tablet has been received and will be erected and unveiled next week."

The entry of June 9, 1949, reads:

"The memorial tablet was erected and unveiled today at 3pm in the presence of the Secondary pupils, the staff of the whole school, and a considerable congregation of relatives of the fallen and others interested. Mr Craigen, Kirkton, who lost two sons in the last war, unveiled the memorial. Major Shaw Mackenzie of Newhall delivered the address and Rev J.B. Russel conducted the dedicatory service. Dr G.G. Middleton, Davidston, presided.

THE 1950's

No one writing about the past is free from the influence of the present; indeed a number of commentators fall into the trap of judging bygone years by the values of the present. This tendency is sometimes evident in the media, when people constantly poke fun — or even sneer — at the values of earlier generations. In dealing with schools in the 1950s, it would be very easy to be unduly critical of that period, for the natural tendency is to write about the fifties with one eye on the eighties, and assume that today, everything we do is right and proper and that the teachers of the 1950s had not yet "seen the light". (It is of course equally possible that the opposite point of view be maintained — that schools are "not what they used to be".)

I myself was a pupil at Stonehaven and progressed through the six years of my secondary education in the 1950s. Adopting the misleading practice of "looking back" from the present, that earlier decade seemed a time of long-accepted ideas existing without challenge: subjects were well-established, all aspects of our pupil/teacher relationship were long entrenched and punishments for wrong-doing — whether standing outside a room or accepting a few strokes of the belt — were accepted as a permanent feature of school life. This is very much an eighties view of the fifties, but, in discussion with several others who were secondary pupils in the fifties, that period does seem to have been a time of relative stability in Scottish schools. The 1960s saw a number of important developments in our society and in our schools, from which, in the 1970s and 1980s, were to come, in quick succession almost overwhelming waves of wide ranging changes of all kinds.

MRS. MACLEMAN

Mrs Macleman, or rather Janice Mackay, as she then was, had actually spent some of her Primary years at Fortrose Academy, and did not therefore feel the impact of the change to secondary schooling as strongly as some others new to Fortrose. In the early 1950s, the feeder areas of Fortrose Academy were nothing like as numerous as they are today, for some areas which might now expect to send their pupils to Fortrose then despatched them to Dingwall. In those years too, a number of secondary pupils attended the schools at Avoch and Cromarty. Mrs Macleman remembers that those early secondary days seemed to pass more quickly than had been the case in Primary School, for the day was broken up into periods which lasted 45 minutes, period changes being signalled by the janitor ringing a large hand-bell!

Mrs Macleman referred to a number of most important differences between the fifties and the sixties — one being the time at which pupils chose their certificate courses. Pupils in the 1980s expect to discuss their course options during their second year, making their decisions in good time to begin their 'O' Grades or 'S' Grades at the start of 3R. This was not the case in the 1950s, for such decisions were taken a year later. There were no 'O' Grades of course, these appearing in the early 1960s, pupils instead sitting "Lowers" in their fifth year. Passing one's "Highers", which could also be taken in the fifth year, had the same high prestige as success in these exams has today. If pupils were sufficiently able, they sat their 'Highers' in the fifth year, and did not concern themselves with 'Lowers' in these subjects. Both grades of examination were taken around March, thereby giving senior pupils the prospect of a pleasant Easter Holiday, a time pupils today cannot enjoy so much, for their certificate examinations start shortly after the Easter break. Mrs Macleman herself took certificate courses in English, Maths, Arithmetic, Latin, French, German and History. She remembers that everyone was taught General Science up to the end of the 3rd year; she also recalls that, in the 1950s, some subjects were still very much "boys only" or "girls only" — woodwork and cookery respectively being two examples, neither of which continued in Fortrose into the senior years. P.E., as we call the subject today, was undertaken in the Drill Hall, Hockey in the town's playing fields, and dancing classes, just before the Christmas Party, were held in the canteen. (ie. in one of the huts at the back of the school.)

Everyone remembers, probably more clearly than anything else, those happy times at the school dance or party, especially the Senior Dance. Even in the 1950s, teachers might be seen by their pupils in a different light, "letting their hair down", and getting into the spirit of the dances with an enthusiasm that would amaze our 1980s "teenagers". Some of the dances would bewilder the pupils of today, such have been the changes on this scene. How many pupils today could master the Quickstep or the Slow Foxtrot, not to mention the Red River Valley? Many other attractions of the senior dance could be long discussed — opportunities perhaps for some pupils to dance with their 'idols' on the staff, or for some shy senior lad to "chat-up" (or was that a sixties' phrase?) that beautiful blonde in the fifth year; then perhaps would chances for pupil gossip about the staff receive considerable stimulus — "Did you see the way Mr X was always smiling at Miss Y?" For the boys, weighty decisions had to be made: who was to be their partner for the refreshments? Who was to be their partner for that famous last waltz? Even in the 1950s, there were a fortunate few senior boys who had managed to persuade their parents to part with the family car for that evening — the ultimate in status symbols! Other poor souls had to walk their girlfriends home, provided they lived within a reasonable distance. All these thoughts (and others) were sparked off when looking at photographs of Fortrose Academy dances and parties of the late 1950s. We are very fortunate in having a good selection of these pictures, some of which are shown here. They are very interesting, for they show a large number of staff and pupils on those happy occasions nearly 30 years ago.

Mrs Macleman recalls that Mr MacPhail was a most efficient Rector, who, apart from his responsibilities in school administration, also taught Latin, Greek, some History and even Maths — for he took charge of a group of pupils who found Lower Maths hard-going. Mrs Macleman modestly adds that she was in that last named group! As a pupil in the 1950s, Mrs Macleman saw the arrival of two teachers who were to stay at the school until their retirement. Mr A.G. Mackenzie came to take the place of Miss Bowie. Miss Bowie had been taken ill while returning from her Christmas Holidays in England, and was admitted to the City Hospital, Edinburgh on 5th January, 1953. Not long afterwards, a phone call to Fortrose conveyed the sad news that Miss Bowie had died. Her influence on her pupils had been considerable; our contributors of her time remember her clearly, speaking highly of her gifts in teaching English. She also had a keen interest in History, and had carried out a great deal of her own research in local history. Unfortunately, this work seems to be lost.

The young Mr Mackenzie, who came to take over the teaching of English proved a most worthy successor; Mrs Macleman remembers his arrival (she was still in her first year) and his teaching style which was clearly efficient — for she can still recite passages of Shakespeare which she learned over thirty years ago! The other young teacher, who arrived when Mrs Macleman was in her second year, was none other than Mr D.W. Macleod, who taught her Geography. Teachers would hand out "lines" as a punishment, and Mrs Macleman apparently did her fair share for Mr Macleod. Both Mr Mackenzie and Mr Macleod were, she recalls, teachers in whose classes pupils could enjoy their education in an atmosphere that was relaxed yet encouraged hard work. A number of teachers had no room of their own, and had to use whatever accommodation was available; as we shall see, Mr D.W. Macleod had this problem to face in his early years teaching at Fortrose, and Mrs Macleman remembers Latin classes in the Woodwork room, Cookery room and even the canteen. Her advanced sixth year work was always in the canteen.

Discipline in the 1950's continued to be strict and the use of the strap was not unusual. Standards of behaviour and dress were clearly set and understood by all. There is, almost certainly, no aspect of school life more fiercely debated today than the question of "deterioration" in discipline in our schools. It is easy to understand why people who were pupils up to the 1960 period, today think that discipline has deteriorated — in those schools once considered "good" schools. When such people see pupils chatting easily and joking with teachers in the street, when they hear pupils arguing their case with some adult perhaps, or openly challenging the wisdom of past generations, they naturally recall their own days in school when they always spoke to a teacher with great respect, or were pleased if a teacher acknowledged their presence!

In Fortrose Academy major changes have taken place in pupil-teacher relationships. Many would agree with Mrs Macleman in saying that in school generally, those relationships today are much better; of course pupils question things more readily, give their views more openly, and expect a reasoned explanation for what goes on in the world. This is as it should be, for pupils must all develop the confidence to discuss — in public — the matters which will affect their lives; the abilities to speak easily and to debate, to influence and make decisions are most important, for people who have these abilities more than ever tend to dominate our lives. Participation in discussion by all must surely therefore be encouraged from an early age.

Making the music!
Mr Goodall is shown in this picture. Although not shown, he would almost certainly be accompanied by Mr Matthewson, (violin) and Mrs MacPhail. (Piano).

At table further from the camera: Facing the camera are: Rector, Mr MacPhail; Mrs Goodall; Mrs MacPhail (no relation of Rector); Mrs S. Mackenzie. Also at that table are Mr Goodall; Mr Matthewson; Mrs MacPhail. Miss Munro and Mr A.G. Mackenzie are at the table in the foreground.

An early 1960s picture, showing, from left to right: James Riddoch; Avril Ross; Jack Sutherland; Irene Barnes; Finlay Matheson; Alison Crawford; Evelyn Fraser; Peter Fraser.

The Christmas Parties — around 1960.

EXTRACTS FROM
THE RECTOR'S LOG BOOK
MISCELLANEOUS MATTERS: 1905-55

26 Sept. 1905 : Experimental Science was commenced today for the first time, as the Laboratory and apparatus have now been got ready for use.

20 May 1910 : Royal Proclamation declared this day to be observed as a day of National Mourning for King Edward VII.

2 March 1915 : Miss MacAndrew's classes have gone into new classroom today. Find sun very strong on south windows and consider blinds should be provided. H.G. classes have also gone into other new classroom. Everything working smoothly.

(This extract refers to the famous "Tin Temple" as it was sometimes called.)

13 Jan. 1922 : School caps were issued to the boys of both departments. They appear to be much valued.

4 Sept. 1925 : Shorthand and Typewriting have been added to the scheme of work of the Post. Int. Division. A Typewriter has been provided by the Authority.

8 Dec. 1925 : A very successful concert was given in the Drill Hall last night by the Secondary Choir and other school music pupils. Exhibitions of Aesthetic Dancing by school pupils were a feature of the entertainment.

18 Oct. 1933 : The collection of geological specimens made by the late Mr Laverie, Rector of the Academy from 1877 to 1913, has been presented to the school.

15 June 1934 : Dr Philip authorised the purchase of a Dutch hoe for the janitor to keep the school yard free of weeds. He also advised the purchase of some weed killer, which has been done.

30 Nov. 1934 : Wednesday was observed as Parents' Day. An invitation was sent thro' the children to parents to visit the school, and considerable advantage was taken of it by mothers to visit the classrooms and see their children actually at work.

11 Jan. 1935 : This week a class of cookery for boys has been arranged.

2 Nov. 1945 : Potato crop in the school garden was completely lifted and stored for use by the school.

16 June 1947 : The Rector was absent from school on Thursday and Friday, attending the Annual General Meeting of the Educational Institute of Scotland where he was installed Vice President for 1947-48.

25 June 1948 : This week the Highland and Agricultural Society held their first post war show in Inverness, and their Majesties the King and Queen were present on Thursday and Friday. In consequence the attendance of the school fell to 81.7% of the roll, large numbers of children having been granted leave to attend the show with their parents. On Thursday afternoon the Scouts and Guides connected with the school proceeded on official duties to Beaufort Castle and the school was closed at 2pm.

11 Feb. 1952 : The school marched to the Town Cross this morning to hear the proclamation of Elizabeth as Queen. The weather was bitterly cold but the children appeared intensely interested in the ceremony.

15 Dec. 1954 : Yesterday evening Miss C.M. Kemp was honoured by parents, former pupils and staff when she received a silver tea-service and a cheque in appreciation of her 46 years' devoted service in the school. The Provost, Dr J.R. Anderson, was in the chair, the presentation being made by Mrs Anderson.

23 Dec. 1955 : The trees along Academy Street have been polled in order to admit more light into the rooms that run parallel to the road. A tall elm near the gate was felled as its branches were beginning to drop: the tree was found to be rotting in the centre.

"11th February, 1952: The proclamation of Elizabeth as Queen."
On the platform can be seen, from the left: Mr MacDowall, Town Clerk; Canon Dobson; Provost John Anderson; Mr Rowat; Police Sergeant Henderson; and an army representative from Fort George.

PHYSICAL EDUCATION

Accommodation difficulties feature frequently in the history of the school, but can seldom be as severe as those faced by some teachers in the department we now call Physical Education. The main problem for many years was simply that there was no gymnasium! Many of our contributors can remember gym classes being held in the Territorial Hall — the Drill Hall, for many years. (This building later became the McKerchar Hall and is now the Roman Catholic Church). Under such circumstances, 'gym' lessons must clearly have been very basic. Mr R. McRae can remember that an itinerant teacher, Miss Davidson, took his class for gym in the Drill Hall for about one hour per week. At that time — the 1920s — Miss Davidson took girls and boys for gym, but in separate groups. There was little in the way of specialist equipment in the hall, but Mr McRae can remember two ropes for climbing. Certainly hockey for girls was very popular, as we have seen, and so too was football for the boys, as we shall presently read.

In spite of all the difficulties of these early years, there was no lack of enthusiasm for sport from either staff or pupils. Mr R. McRae remembers that, in the 1920s, Mr Matheson, a Maths teacher who sometimes also taught English, was a great sports enthusiast. He ran a football team that was able to beat any other team in the area. By good luck, one of the many photographs which have been given to the History Department is of this well remembered football team. Equally fortunate is the fact that two of the team's members now live nearby, and these brothers agreed most willingly to provide information about the picture. Mr D. Sutherland, Rosemarkie and Mr A. Sutherland, Fortrose, remember their school football team very clearly. A photograph of this team is shown opposite/overleaf. The pupils involved are:

Back row: (Left to right): L. MacDonald, a pupil from Cromarty, and nominal trainer; Adam Ritchie; William Cooper; William Goodall; Alec McFarlane.

Middle row: Roddy Fraser; A Sutherland; D. Sutherland, Captain; Hamish (or James) Anderson; Hector Cameron.

Front row: Magnus Urquhart; Charlie Cameron.

The team was made up from 4th, 5th, and 6th year pupils. The school colours were black and red. Mr Matheson, the teacher who organised matches, and acted as referee, actually took the photograph. A coloured enlargement of the picture was placed above the fireplace in the Rector's room. The young Sutherland brothers were certainly keen on their football, for, when they arrived at school in the morning, one would climb through a window, which was never snibbed, into the Rector's room to get a football, and they played until 9am! It was interesting to hear that, coming to Fortrose Academy from Avoch, the brothers did not normally use Academy Street, but walked along the top of the higher ground above the beach; they passed in front of Mr A. Sutherland's present home, and in front of the Rector's house, and then cut across to the school.

The football team played on many occasions, against other school teams from, for instance, Dingwall Academy or Inverness Royal Academy. The team also played Cromarty Thistle and Fortrose Union; on every outing the team actually won — they never merely drew a match. Transport was clearly no problem to these enthusiasts; the train was used where possible, and Hastie's bus, with its well remembered ticket collector "Hattie", provided transport to Cromarty. When playing "at home", they used the field in front of the school, or the King George V park for playing Fortrose Union.

Both Mr A Sutherland and Mr D Sutherland remember using the Territorial Hall for "Drill"; they never used a room in the school. In fact, their gym lessons, taken by Miss Davidson, were held only once per month!

Messrs. D and A Sutherland today, standing on the route which they often used to come to school in the 1920s.
As you can see, the ground behind them, once wide enough to take a large cart, has been considerably eroded.

Certainly there had been concern for some years at the lack of a gym in Fortrose Academy, and attempts were made to do something to provide one. In October 1914, there had been correspondence with the Scotch Education Department to secure permission to have a classroom altered and made suitable for use as a gymnasium. One plan of the school, dated 1914, actually shows one classroom as "converted into gymnasium". The fact that this room was surrounded by three other classrooms would have made its use as a gym, for however short a period in the week, really quite unsuitable for many activities. Other problems in the use of a classroom as a gym readily come to mind; nevertheless, the room was used for some time at least, as Miss Young and Mrs J.M. Mackenzie both remember.

Members of staff who are former pupils have many memories of gym and games in their pupil days. Miss E. MacLeod recalls that when she was a pupil, the girls enjoyed netball outside the school, and that Miss Holm, not herself a gym teacher, took hockey. Miss E. MacLeod was herself a member of the senior girls hockey team. One day when she was not able to play, she was asked instead to prepare a lunch for the visiting team. The Rector in fact directed that fish and chips would be served! Fortunately, Miss MacLeod secured the help of a kindly member of the canteen staff, who prepared the meal, leaving Miss MacLeod with the easier task of actually serving it to her fellow pupils.

Mr H. Patience, recalling his days as a pupil at Fortrose Academy, remembers that the field in front of the school (ie. where the present 'new' buildings are, eg. the assembly hall, staff room area etc.) was still used by pupils for games. The grass was never actually cut, but was sufficiently flattened by the pupils — except after the summer holidays when it had grown quite high. He also confirmed that all gym was taught in the Drill Hall, right up to the time when the new buildings went up in the mid sixties. It occasionally happened that the Drill Hall might not be available for school use. There were a number of reasons for this: the hall might be closed for redecorating work, its heating system might have failed, or it might simply be needed by other groups.

Sports Days have always been enjoyed by participants and spectators alike. The Rector's Log Book records this comment of that day in June 1951:

> "The Secondary School Sports were held on Wednesday, 20th June, and the Primary School Sports on Thursday, 21st June at 2pm. There was a larger number of parents and friends than last year. The weather on both afternoons was fine and the Union Park was in good condition. Unfortunately two secondary pupils sustained injuries during the High Jump competitions. Both pupils were attended at once by Dr Chrystal and afterwards sent to Inverness for X-ray and medical attention."

It should be made clear that for most of the period covered by this magazine, PE teachers were involved with schools other than Fortrose Academy, although they would regard this school as their centre. It must have therefore been with considerable joy that Mr MacPhail welcomed a deputation of S.E.D. and County Architects around the end of June, 1958: these visitors had arrived to inspect the school and its grounds with a view to the erection of new buildings — to include gym accommodation! Sadly the time when a gymnasium would be built was still some years away, as we now know.

Although still without proper accommodation, PE teachers clearly put great effort not only into teaching their pupils, but into developing their subject. The term "P.T." (Physical Training) was disappearing from general use and the use of the letters "P.E." — "Physical Education" was becoming much more popular to indicate a much broader approach to the subject. (It must be said, however, that this latter term had been used in the Rector's Log Book as far back as 1914).

A cheerful hockey team! (Around 1960.) Left to right: **Back row:** *Alison Crawford, Jane Reid, Janis Smith, Sheila Ross, Rae McIntosh.* **Front row:** *Isobel Reid, Evelyn Fraser, Irene Barnes, Joan Cameron, Mary Marwick. Teacher: Miss Turnbull.*

The school playing fields, photographed in the summer term, 1987. As you can see, many pupils are using them — and it wasn't a "Sports day" either!

By the early 1960s too, the "House" system was well established in Fortrose Academy, and this certainly further stimulated the interest and enthusiasm of all in the school's various sporting activities. An article in the 1963 edition of the school magazine is particularly interesting, for not only does it describe a very close and exciting sports day finish, but it also refers to the existence of four houses. The article, written by Evan Sutherland, then a pupil in the second year, and later a head boy of the school, is well worth quoting in full:

> "I shall never forget the dramatic finish to last year's school sports in Fortrose Academy. The four houses, McIntosh, Urquhart, Mackenzie and Miller, were locked together with ninety points each. The last event, the high jump, was coming to an end, with only the Miller and McIntosh representatives remaining. The bar had steadily risen inch by inch. Both boys were jumping brilliantly. Suddenly — calamity for Miller House! Their representative, who had failed in his first two attempts, slipped at his last effort. The McIntosh champion succeeded in clearing the hurdle. Thus concluded a magnificent sporting day for my school, especially McIntosh House."

One of the House names listed above was soon to be withdrawn, leaving Miller, McIntosh and Mackenzie. There is no need to explain the choice of these names, for they were people with well known Black Isle connections, James McIntosh being one of the school's most famous former pupils. The names were to last for some years. In the late 1970s, however, it was felt that new house names should be introduced. Mr L. Murdoch's suggestion that the Houses (four again) should have the names Boniface, Duthac, Martin and Regulus, was taken up by the staff for a number of reasons, one being that these names, each with a different initial letter, and sounding (and looking) quite distinct from each other, would be much more easily understood in recording sports events. Mr Murdoch recalls that the Boniface Fair reappeared in the year he came to Fortrose and that this colourful event probably set his mind thinking along the lines of saints with local connections.

57

This brief comment on the history of the P.E. Department can be brought to an end on a happy note regarding the provision of a gymnasium. The two P.E. teachers of the time must have been delighted to see the new buildings go up in the mid-sixties, for, at last, there appeared a gymnasium, with changing rooms and showers included. The early 1970s saw the building of further extensions to the Academy, including a much needed second gymnasium. One other most significant development must be recorded — the acquisition of the school's playing fields, which were a most welcome addition to the school. In this connection, the work of Mr Duncan McPherson must be most gratefully acknowledged.

The lists of teams which were successful over the years would fill a great deal of space. Many photographs held in the school exist as a tribute to pupils' skills. Here is one picture of the school's badminton team of the early 1970s. The team enjoyed tremendous success and included over the years a number of pupils not shown here. The pupils are, left to right:
Back row: Colin Campbell; Ian Thompson; Alastair Cameron; Guy Vaughan.
Front row: Isobel MacAngus; Christine Wilkins; Fiona MacDonald — who was later to be Principal Teacher of P.E. in the school, leaving in October 1987 to take up a position as a lecturer in Physical Education. The teacher in charge of the team is Mr W. Campbell who retired in the mid 70s.

Fortrose Academy enjoyed notable successes in a variety of sports and drew much favourable comment in the Press.

The Principal Teacher of P.E. during these years was Mr. J. Sutherland, a former pupil of the school.

This is a most interesting picture of a Sports day around 1930. Rector, Mr K. Macleod is seen clearly, facing the camera and Mrs Macleod is presenting the prizes. The Rev. Mr Craig is seated close to the table, with Mr Fleming, retired headmaster at Avoch, beside him.

Sports Day, 10th June, 1987. A section of the crowd eagerly awaits the announcement of the winning house. Miss MacDonald, Principal Teacher of P.E. can just be seen near the tent, next to the Assistant Rector, Mr Ferguson, who had recently arrived at the school.

EXTRACTS FROM
THE RECTOR'S LOG BOOK
ABSENCE from SCHOOL: 1950-55
ILLNESS, BAD WEATHER and POTATO LIFTING!

29 Sept. 1950 : Potato lifting has started and exemptions amounting to 42 attendances and involving six pupils have been granted. Warning has been given to the pupils of IA, IIA, III, IV and V of the extremely prejudicial effects of three weeks' absence on their studies; pupils who help on their parents' farms have been warned to reduce their absences to a minimum.

13 Oct. 1950 : The mumps epidemic is now spreading through the Primary School, about nine pupils now being infected. In addition six contacts are being excluded.

30 Oct. 1950 : The potato-harvest is at present in full swing. Classes IIB and IB have shrunk very considerably and Class IIB has therefore been joined to IIA most of the week. The level of attendance in IA, IIA and III is reasonably satisfactory and work progresses as usual.

3 Nov. 1950 : Mumps seems to be very rife in the locality at present after a quiescent period of a few weeks.

4 Dec. 1950 : Owing to the heavy snowfall during the week-end attendance was lower than usual. Mumps still continues to smoulder in the primary and junior secondary classes.

22 Dec. 1950 : The attendance of the last three weeks has been badly affected by the exceptionally wintry conditions prevailing in the countryside. Buses were often late and many pupils, especially in the Primary School, were unable to make their way through the deep snow from their homes to the main roads. The Cromarty bus on Tuesday, 19th Dec., arrived 1½ hours late while on Monday, 18th Dec., the Avoch pupils waited in vain for their bus and reached school on foot about 9.30 a.m.

Mumps continues to affect the attendance; it is almost assuming the nature of an endemic disease. Work has been very badly affected in the lower classes of the Primary School where its toll has been heaviest.

12 Jan. 1951 : The attendance this week remained very low at 81.3%. The weather has continued to be very frosty, roads are snowbound or dangerously icy. Most of the absences, however, were caused by the prevailing influenza. There are at least three cases of mumps in the Secondary School.

2 March 1951 : Owing to the improvement in the weather the attendance reached the percentage of 93.6, the highest since September.

23 Oct. 1951 : For the last fortnight classes II and III have been seriously affected by potato-lifting exemptions. Class IIB has completely disappeared while IA has lost a third of its strength. Two girls who absented themselves from Class IV have been warned of the consequences to their studies. The general state of suspended animation caused by potato-lifting is disastrous in its immediate and remote effects.

25 Jan. 1952	: The roads have been ice-bound for more than 3 weeks now. Buses often fail to maintain their time-tables with the result that all the pupils are not present at 9 o'clock. Attendance especially in the primary school, has been affected by the weather.
9 June 1952	: Two girls were excluded on account of suspected German measles.
17 Jan. 1955	: Owing to the abnormally heavy snowfalls of the last week attendance has been very poor. The Cromarty bus was unable to make its way through to Newhall today; all pupils from that area are therefore absent.
21 Jan. 1955	: This week has witnessed one of the hardest frosts and heaviest snowfalls for some years. Attendance was 61%, many of the children from outlying farms being unable to reach the main roads. An influenza epidemic appears to be raging in the Cromarty area.
17 Feb. 1955	: Considerably less than 50% of the pupils being present, the school was closed at 1 p.m. and a double attendance marked.
18 Feb. 1955	: As the roads to Rosemarkie, Avoch and Killen were blocked by snow-drifts only pupils from Fortrose were in attendance at 9am. These pupils were sent home and the school closed for the day at 9.15am.
1 March 1955	: The thaw has started and is proceeding rapidly. For the first time for many weeks the attendance is almost normal. Until now attendance has been kept abnormally low by the two snowfalls and a smouldering epidemic of colds, influenza, etc. In addition, sporadic cases of measles, mumps, and even scarlet fever have been reported.

◄ ○ ►

THE 1960's

The 1960's were eventful years in the history of our school, and this magazine concentrates on the major building developments of that decade. There were, of course, many other newsworthy items, and there is no better way to introduce the sixties than to quote in full the "School News" contained in the Fortrose Academy Magazine of June, 1960.

"SCHOOL NEWS

("I will a round unvarnished tale deliver.")

Editorial commands must be obeyed, and we have strict instructions to be brief. Stylish flourishes are therefore eschewed.

In our last edition of this magazine, we bade farewell to Mr MacDonald, teacher of Modern Languages. In August, we welcomed his successor, Mr Campbell, who came to us from Glasgow High School. Already Mr Campbell has proved himself "School News" worthy. He has introduced a French Magazine "Dis-Donc"; he has, in co-operation with Mr Greig, organised a Chess Club which is extremely popular; and he was married during the Easter holidays. The pupils presented him with a crystal bowl, and gave him a rousing send-off. He also received a present from the staff. We wish Mr Campbell and his wife all happiness for the future.

Another departure from the Academy — this time from the Junior School — is to be noted. In November, Miss MacLennan, the Infant Mistress, left us to go to South Africa. There was great sadness among the infants, and indeed throughout the whole school, for Miss MacLennan was an extremely popular lady with all pupils and staff of the Academy. Her marriage in Johannesburg was reported in the "Ross-shire Journal".

Miss MacLennan's place in the Infant Room has been taken over by Mrs Mackenzie, and Primary 3 and 4 classes are being taught by Mrs MacLeod.

We take this opportunity of extending a belated but nevertheless warm welcome to our new school chaplain, the Rev. Alexander Macrae B.D., who is Mr Craig's successor in the Church of Scotland, Fortrose.

Changes in the appearance of the school have also taken place. East of the canteen a new building has been erected, consisting of two classrooms and a spacious storeroom. After years of dodging about the school, for all the world like book-salesmen, Miss Urquhart and Mr MacLeod have, with profound sighs of relief, taken occupation of Rooms 10 and 11 respectively.

A new electric bell system has been installed in the school. No cry of "To the Lifeboats" could ever have the effect that those bells have.

During the first term, the school was honoured by a visit from the Moderator of the General Assembly of the Church of Scotland, the Rev. Dr. Shepherd, who gave a most interesting address on work of the Church in Africa, and particularly of his own experience in that country.

Another speaker who talked to the senior pupils at Morning Service was Dr. Sloane, who spoke of the work of the Mission to Lepers.

Last June senior pupils had a delightful day's outing to the West Coast, an account of which is given elsewhere in the Magazine. June 29th has been settled as the day for this year's picnic and that is a date we look forward to with the utmost eagerness.

We wish success (and a lot of fun, too) to the Hockey team which is going to cross the Minch on June 24th to play the Nicolson Institute's XI.

Finally we express our very best wishes to all those who are working so hard just now for the School Concert. Under Mr Greig's direction Academy concerts have achieved a considerable reputation for excellence in the past. We hear whispers that the forthcoming concert on June 22nd and 23rd is even more ambitious than previous efforts. We look forward to it. Good luck to all concerned.

Fiona Crawford V."

Mr MacPhail.
Rector 1949-72

HITTING THE HEADLINES!
THE PRIZE-GIVING CEREMONY, JULY 1960

The Fortrose Academy prize-giving of 1st July, 1960, was held in the Town Hall. There was a large audience. There were also large headlines in "The Press and Journal" the following day, for Mr MacPhail's speech, along with the comments of two other Highland Rectors, provided the main front page story of that newspaper on Saturday, 2nd July, 1960.

There is no doubt that Mr MacPhail's speech was a most courageous one. In the 1980s, we have become accustomed to reading of Rectors' speeches which are critical of local authority educational provision; in fact, such speeches have become quite frequent. We must remember that this was most certainly not the case in 1960, and Mr MacPhail's outspoken criticisms must therefore have had a very considerable impact.

"The Press and Journal" reported Mr MacPhail's speech in detail, and quite rightly so, for it was to be an important stage in the Rector's struggle for new accommodation. The Rector's protests came at a date when government policy in such matters was soon to switch from "stop" to "go". Whether the fortunate timing of the speech was luck or judgement is not certain, but people who knew Mr MacPhail think it was almost without doubt judgement of a fine kind!

"The Press and Journal" has kindly given permission for its report to be quoted and below are given the details relating to Mr MacPhail's speech.

3 HEADS HIT OUT
Education Bodies Get a Caning....

Headmasters of three schools in the North and North-east made outspoken attacks on their education authorities in prize-giving speeches yesterday.

Mr W.D. MacPhail, Rector of Fortrose Academy, attacked the inadequacy of his school buildings and warned: "Until we are provided with the prescribed accommodation, we cannot progress — we can only mark time."

He said that during his stay at Fortrose he had suffered more frustration from poverty of accommodation than from any other single factor.

Mr MacPhail said that few members of the general public seemed to be aware of the handicaps under which they laboured at Fortrose.

Their art room was a corrugated iron structure erected in 1914. Their library was housed in the basement of the bell tower. Their science laboratory was a "museum piece". There was no janitor's room. He and his stores occupied what was intended to be a science experiment room. The men teachers' staff room was only slightly bigger — 10ft by 9ft — and had to accommodate eight teachers.

BACK IN 1911
"During the mercifully infrequent visitations of the medical officer and school dentist the lady teachers require to be ejected from their staff room because we have no medical inspection room. There is no assembly hall," said Mr MacPhail.

The drill hall was used for physical education. The school log book disclosed that in 1911, when the grandparents of some of the present pupils were at school, the inspectorate recommended to the old Rosemarkie School Board that a "modest gymnasium" be erected at Fortrose.

The modest gymnasium was never erected. Instead recourse was had to the drill hall, which was roundly condemned by the inspectorate as far back as 1933 and repeatedly since then, because it had no dressing rooms, no lavatories, no showers, no fixed equipment.

The teachers, he said, are forbidden to allow the children to play ball games in case the paint on the wall is damaged. The hall was situated about 200 yards from the school so that at least five minutes were spent each way in walking, sometimes in adverse weather.

COLD COMFORT

Nowadays, said Mr MacPhail, a teacher of physical education who was not provided with a gymnasium was being asked to make bricks without straw.

"One is almost driven to despair by the knowledge that the Scottish Education Department has permitted its inspectorate's recommendation to be flouted by successive governing bodies for forty-nine years.

"It is cold comfort to be told that Fortrose must take its place in the queue, since all Ross-shire mainland secondary schools outside Dingwall suffer from similar or even worse deficiencies. The stark inference to be drawn from this statement is that approximately two out of three secondary school children are denied their rightful educational amenities.

"Four out of five senior secondary schools on the Ross-shire mainland lack the cardinal amenities of a standard gymnasium, an assembly hall and a library room. The position in primary schools is almost certainly worse.

SOCIAL JUSTICE

"I hope that nobody grudges Dingwall the magnificent facilities now enjoyed by its school, but why are the same facilities not extended to all Ross-shire schools?

"It is surely an axiom of social justice that, where all parents pay the same rates to the same authority, pupils and teachers should receive the same facilities within that authority's area.

"I believe that the intentions of the planning authorities are excellent", said Mr MacPhail, "but their unconscionable delays often make me wonder whether they realise how extremely short childhood is. During my eleven years of rectorship three generations of junior secondary pupils and two generations of senior secondary pupils have been denied the facilities to which they had imprescriptible right.

"It is a chastening reflection that, unless a massive carefully-planned assault is mounted at once on obsolescent buildings and carried through with the shock of a military operation, none of our present secondary pupils, and possibly few of our primary pupils, will enjoy the accommodation which the Education Department prescribes.

"The days are long since departed when a shelf of books and a brace of test tubes in a one-roomed school were sufficient to prepare the lad of parts for the university".

An early 1960's staff photograph. From the left
Back row: Mr Patience; Mr McCuish; Mr R. Laing; Mr Greig; Mr A. Campbell; Mr MacIntyre; Mr MacDonald; Mr Goodall; Mr Macleod.
Front row: Miss Murray; Mrs Brown; Mrs MacAdam; Mr MacPhail; Mr Mackenzie; Mrs Miller; Miss Whyte; Mrs Mackenzie.

MR M. KIRKWOOD: ARCHITECT

No doubt many people have driven along the main road from Muir of Ord to Beauly and beyond and have glanced westwards towards the nearby higher ground which looks so pleasant. I recently had the chance to find out just how attractive that hilly area is, for I was using its quiet road on my way to visit a croft at Broallan, Kilmorack. This is the home of Mr Kirkwood, who worked for many years in the Ross and Cromarty County Architect's Department in Dingwall. This department had been most ably developed by its leader Mr Leask. It was Mr Kirkwood who was given the responsibility for the architectural planning of the major work that was to take place at Fortrose Academy in the mid 1960s.

To someone who had spent his boyhood days in the countryside in the forties and fifties, a most pleasant scene presented itself as I approached Mr Kirkwood's home, for on one side of his house, the corn had just been cut, sheaved and stooked! Another field of corn had been attended to that day, the work not quite finished. In the middle of the field stood a 1956 Ferguson tractor, with its familiar grey appearance, and attached to it a Canadian built, Deering number Three Binder. The sheaves lay on the ground, about to be put into stooks. Altogether a fascinating picture, especially to someone who remembered such scenes in the north-east as the norm in his childhood days. In fact Mr Kirkwood had owned the tractor for many years, for he had bought it when it was less than a year old. Thirty years later, it still gives good service! Equally interesting was a small threshing mill, for it had been made in Dingwall in the days when such machines would have been built specifically for the needs of particular farms in the area. Walking towards the front door of the house, I stopped to admire two 1960s Volvo cars. One, which was kept for spares, was a 1966 model which had covered 160,000 miles!

FORTROSE ACADEMY: THE MID 1960s
THE NEW BUILDINGS GO UP!

No architect is given a free hand in the design of a school! The Scottish Education Department gives a detailed description of requirements for new school buildings and all the work must be done within the given financial limits. Clearly the S.E.D. has a strong influence, and its architects' department in Edinburgh will scrutinise very closely all plans drawn up by the local authority staff. The Rector of a school involved also sends in specific requirements. The local architect in charge has several further considerations which must be taken into account; the amount of land available, and its cost, will clearly have an important effect on the design of a new school; there are many legal aspects to be taken into account, regulations dealing with fire precautions being a good example. Of the subjects taught in the school, many require specialist accommodation, and this will have to be studied; clearly a gymnasium cannot be placed on the top floor and surrounded by classrooms! Materials and methods of construction have to be decided, taking into account many factors such as cost efficiency, maintenance, structural safety and soundproofing. The floor areas of classrooms are specified too. There are a number of plans for the "mid-sixties" buildings in the school, different sets dealing with different aspects of the school. They illustrate the fact that the construction of a school is a very complex business indeed.

When the time came for new building developments at Fortrose in the 1960s, a very important decision had to be taken at the outset; should the school then on the site be completely demolished and an all-new building erected, or should the buildings already there be included,

68

even if this meant extensive alteration? Careful consideration was given to this matter and designs were studied for a completely new school.

The decision was taken — most of the buildings of the 'old' school would be kept. Many then felt and today still feel that this was without any doubt the correct decision, for the contrasting styles of different periods add a visual interest to a school which all new structures lack. The photograph below, taken in 1987, shows the attractive appearance of the school.

That decision was arrived at only after many hours had been spent in studying the ways in which the old buildings were to be used (and therefore what then must be included in the new buildings), and on the vital question of how and where old and new buildings were to meet.

As we know today, these problems were tackled most successfully. Externally the marriage of old and new was achieved most effectively. Internally the problem was mastered to produce not only an attractive feature of the school, but a most useful dual-purpose area. The space occupied for long by the school's science room was transformed and became the stage. The decision had been taken to use other classrooms nearby as the new school kitchen area, for their ceiling height, and other factors, made them particularly suitable; two rooms beside the new kitchen made a most useful canteen area, particularly so in that the new stage could be used as an overflow area during the lunch hour. A sliding partition was placed between the canteen and the stage so that either could be used entirely as a separate unit. A new assembly hall was built out from the stage, at a level well below it.

The main entrance hall at the back of the assembly hall is also a dual-purpose area. Fitted with a folding partition, part can be used most effectively as the balcony of the assembly hall. The main passageway along the side of the hall can be used for the same purpose, and passing as it does on the east side of the stage, gives extra space in that area. This main corridor then joins the main corridor of the 'old' building opposite the entrance bay to the one gymnasium which was part of the mid-sixties additions.

Altogether, the areas of the school kitchens, canteen, stage, assembly and entrance halls operate today most effectively; the use of the assembly hall as the link between old and new has been entirely successful.

The meeting of old and new.

How many pupils realise, as they devour their chosen meal of the day on the stage, that they are sitting on the area that was once a science room?.... Or that, if they are enjoying their lunch towards the other end of the canteen, that they are in the spaces — in the original school up to 1933 — that formed the Rector's study, the coal store, or the boys' toilets?

The aforementioned gymnasium, with its associated changing rooms and showers, was built well away from the main, new teaching block, as was the new technical education

The canteen. A view from the stage near the end of the lunch hour.

accommodation. (The 'old' school buildings, at right angles to what are now the school kitchens, were demolished to make way for the new technical education wing and of course to provide the open area we see there today). The Primary department was now to be housed in the 'old' buildings towards the east end of the school, in the area now occupied by the technical education drawing and woodwork rooms.

There were other parts of the new school which were constructed away from, or at least on the outer edge of the main, new three storey teaching block. The administration/staff room wing is very well positioned, for it is easily accessible both by visitors coming into the school, and by pupils and staff in the course of their working day. Externally too this wing is attractively designed; people arriving at the main front gate find their eyes naturally directed, by the presence of the blank wall, towards the main entrance, with its mosaic showing the school badge.

Another line of buildings on the Ness side of the main block served a variety of needs. At its east end was a medical inspection room, (planned somewhat later, and now part of the Home Economics Department) then the Home Economics accommodation, a Music Room and at the west end, virtually on its own, the Boiler Room.

The main three storey building takes up a great deal less space than the same amount of accommodation on one floor, and this was clearly one of the main considerations in its design. It is a steel framed building, its steel frame arriving in Fortrose in forty foot lengths — not a common sight in the town! A re-inforced concrete base was prepared for these vertical lengths, which in turn were put in place by a large crane. The chain holding the steel framing would normally slip off easily when so desired; on one occasion it refused to free itself and one construction worker quickly shinned up the vertical steel to free it. The steel frame used in such buildings goes up quickly as many people today will have noticed, having seen such methods used in the building of shopping stores etc. The columns were encased in concrete, using a wooden frame and working from ground level — a process known as "shuttering". Structural engineers Fairhurst and Partners from Glasgow were responsible for the steel work and the re-inforced concrete. The concrete itself had to be prepared to a certain standard; concrete cubes were taken and checked by crushing, a necessary measure to ensure the future safety of the structure. Re-inforced concrete floors were installed, this being needed to provide both strength and sound-proofing. The safety of the building in relation to the danger of fire was also checked most carefully. At the design stage, there was close consultation with the Fire Service in Inverness. The building regulations regarding fire precautions are rightly very strict, and it was essential that the new school should be as safe as it could possibly be in this respect.

Mr Kirkwood remembers clearly the moment the new buildings got under way, for he was on the site when one of Hall's diggers took out the first scoop of soil to prepare the site! After all the work that had gone into the planning, it must have been marvellous to see the paperwork become a reality. Mr Kirkwood visited the site regularly, the actual number of visits per week depending on the work in hand. He could of course be called out to help at any time, and one such occasion stands out in his mind. Summoned by a phone call to Fortrose, he was motoring along (in that Volvo which was to cover 160,000 miles) when he realised that the lump of dried mud or whatever on the road just ahead was in fact a piece of rock or stone! As motorists know, sometimes it is impossible to do anything else but go over such an obstacle and this is what Mr Kirkwood did. Unfortunately, some lower part at the front of the car must have hit it — and in its route along to the back of the car, it left a trail of damage before bouncing away.

The Clerk of Works was on the building site every day to check on the work and he reported on its progress weekly. When the new buildings were completed, the staff and pupils moved in, and work was then possible on the modification of the 'old' building. (The Rector's Log Book records that staff and pupils entered their brand new accommodation on 21st December, 1965).

Teachers had known for some time which rooms they were to occupy. Mr A. MacDonald, Principal Teacher of Technical Education, had given a talk to the P.T.A. on the lay-out of the new school. This had been at a time when plans were finalised, but building had not started. Mr A. MacDonald and his pupils had prepared overhead views of each floor, and cards were

From many of the rooms in the school, the views are superb. Later building, however, took away some pleasant outlooks — this photograph, taken around 1970 from Room 2, illustrating one such example.

provided with details of each room. Members of staff had been most interested to see where they were to teach; their views on many matters had already been considered by the Architects' Department.

It should also be remembered that a janitor's house was included in the list of works undertaken at that time. One final observation must be made — all huts were cleared away, including the famous "Tin Temple". All was now ready for the official opening of the "New Buildings".

This picture shows a close-up view of the tower. The dates shown — 1791, 1891, 1933 and 1967 — refer to important stages in the History of the school, the last three being years of major building on the present site.

THE OFFICIAL OPENING OF
THE NEW BUILDINGS AT FORTROSE ACADEMY
23rd OCTOBER 1967

The "Ross-shire Journal" of Friday 3rd November, 1967, gave a full and most interesting report on the official opening of the new buildings at Fortrose Academy. The History Department is, once again, most grateful to the "Ross-shire Journal" for granting permission to quote from this article.

"The Country Convener, Rev. M.J. Nicolson, Muir of Ord, presided at the ceremony in the splendidly appointed assembly hall, and extended a warm welcome to a gathering of members of the Town and County Councils, staff and pupils of the school, and several parents.

There was one person especially welcome, and that was the former Rector of the Academy, Mr Kenneth Macleod, who is now resident in Inverness.

The Convener said they were indeed delighted to see Mr Macleod. From his own early days he had been taught that the story of Peter Pan was a fable, but now he must come to the conclusion that there was some truth in it after all, when he looked at Mr Macleod!

A marvellous job had been made of the creation and construction of this modern school, he said. When one realised the inadequacy of the previous buildings, and the difficulties under which staff and pupils had to work, it was a tribute to the present Rector and his staff, and to his predecessor, that they produced the scholars they did under the circumstances. What impressed him most, on looking at the school, was the manner in which the architect and builders had been able to combine the old and the new. This was a remarkable feature of the building. It was a symbol of what they hoped for. They wanted all that was best in their tradition — and they had an excellent tradition — and all that was best in their heritage, to be combined with all that was new in the opportunities set before them. The Convener felt confident the effort would be worthwhile.

The Prayer of Dedication was made by the Rev. H.G. Mackay, B.D., Free Church Manse, Killearnan.

MAJOR CAMERON

Introducing Major Allan Cameron, Allangrange, Chairman of the Education Committee, who was to perform the opening ceremony, the Convener said that since Major Cameron had taken over as chairman, he had familiarised himself with the situation existing in every school in the County, and this included the Isle of Lewis. It was through his leadership, determination, sense of urgency, and fairness, that they were now beginning to see things taking shape in the County. It was largely through Major Cameron's efforts, and the encouragement received from Mr Forsyth, Chief Inspector, who were present with them, that the present ceremony was taking place."

Major Cameron went on to give an engaging account of the history of education in this area, including in it a number of humourous stories and comments, and some witty remarks aimed in a number of directions, including the County Buildings at Dingwall. Here is an example of another good natured comment, aimed at the boys' hairstyles of the period....

"Major Cameron pointed out that if any of the company cared to visit Mario's cafe they would see a very gentle-mannered society, and no vice. The only thing the boys required was a haircut, otherwise the scholars of today were all right".

The "Ross-shire Journal" continues:

"IMPROVING THE PAST

Why had he been talking about the past? Major Cameron said he had done so because this was not a brand new school. It was a modernisation scheme. What were bad and inadequate buildings had been pulled down, and what were good and useful were kept and new modern buildings added. It was the same in life. This was how they progressed. They improved on the past, but used the best as a foundation. In Fortrose they had an old school in which they had great pride, and now the pupils could bring credit and distinction on themselves and their new school.

PRIDE IN FORTROSE ACADEMY

The Major extolled the boys and girls to be proud that they were educated at Fortrose, and never let the school down. If they did something stupid it would bring discredit not only on themselves, but also on their school, which had a great tradition, of which they had every right to be proud. He had been honoured to be asked to declare the school open, and he did so, at the same time wishing all who taught and were taught in the school the very best of luck in the future.

One final item, he concluded, after great persuasion Mr MacPhail had agreed to declare a half-holiday next day!"

The reply to Major Cameron's address was given by Mr W.D. MacPhail, the Rector, who also formally accepted the new buildings from the Education Authority. One cannot but feel very glad on Mr MacPhail's behalf for he had fought so hard, and risked considerable censure for his outspoken comments, in order that the pupils could benefit from the building of proper accommodation.

The "Ross-shire Journal" concludes its report with these paragraphs:

"The Head Prefect, Miss Mary Patience, presented Mrs Allan Cameron with a beautiful bouquet of flowers, after which the School's String Orchestra played two delightful pieces.

The votes of thanks to all who were involved in the building of the new Academy, and who had helped in any way to bring the day's events to fruition, were proposed by Mrs A.B.M. Macdonald, Fortrose, a member of the Education Committee.

The Benediction was pronounced by Rev. J.D. Marshall, The Deanery, Fortrose.

Afterwards guests were taken on a tour of the school, and entertained to light refreshments, which were served by the canteen staff, assisted by the senior girls".

THE COUNTY COUNCIL OF ROSS AND CROMARTY EDUCATION COMMITTEE

REQUEST THE PLEASURE OF THE COMPANY OF

AT THE OFFICIAL OPENING OF

THE NEW BUILDINGS AT FORTROSE ACADEMY

BY MAJOR **ALLAN CAMERON,**

CHAIRMAN OF THE EDUCATION COMMITTEE

On MONDAY, 23rd OCTOBER, 1967

AT 3 P.M.

R.S.V.P. TO THE COUNTY CLERK,
COUNTY BUILDINGS, DINGWALL,
BY 16th OCTOBER, 1967.   (A PROGRAMME IS ENCLOSED).

The early 1960's.
From the left: Standing: *James Riddoch — partly visible; Alison Crawford; Clara Crowden; Peter Fraser; Sandy Watson; John MacDonald; Fiona Crawford; Janet Oag; Irene Barnes; Jack Sutherland; ....; Evelyn Fraser; Donald McLeman; William Urquhart; Vincent Bowker.* Seated or kneeling: *Doreen MacLeman; ....; Heather Maclean; Elizabeth Macleay; Eleanor Lindsay; Ian Fraser; Sandy Murcar, Kathleen Jack; Mhairi MacKenzie; Veronica Watson.*

MUSIC

The early 1960's.
From the left: Front row: *Ian Russell; Peter Fraser; Jack Sutherland; James Riddoch; David Munro; Angus MacPhail; Seamus MacPhail.* Back row: *Alistair Reid; Donnie Munro; Victor Thompson; Finlay Maclean.*

Music provides an experience which has a powerful effect not only on all people, but during all stages of their lives. Certainly most of us have enjoyed the pleasure that only music has the power to bestow. With so many aspects it easily captures the imagination of young and old, country or city folk, or rich and poor from any area in the world. These different facets can also be a source of horrific irritation, particularly when one mode of music — not necessarily "pop" — blasts its presence across the streets of our towns and cities, reaching all ears, whether welcome or not. On such occasions, fierce arguments can occur about the respective merits of different styles of music! A hypnotic delight to one, the same music might genuinely be regarded as a form of severe environmental pollution by another. Creating such extremes of feeling, and with such variety of content, Music must be one of the most difficult of school subjects to tackle.

The Music Department at Fortrose Academy had, for many years, to suffer all the problems caused by the complete lack of proper specialist accommodation. In spite of these difficulties, the school did remarkably well in stimulating pupils' interest in music. In conversation with Miss Hay, we heard that, in the twenties, pupils were well known for their singing ability and competed in music festivals. Mr Rod Macrae too, remembers Miss Cameron, the music teacher of that decade, and recalls that she insisted on everything being just right in her music lessons. He mentions that not all boys were too keen on singing solo! Miss Cameron told one boy who could not sing (at that time anyway!) that he would find life hard if he was unable to appreciate music. He later turned out to be a great dancing enthusiast.

The Music Department faced a number of other problems, including, for some time, the lack of a proper Music teacher. At such a time the teaching of Music ceased. When the Music teacher resigned on March 1st. 1951, it took some time to secure a replacement! The Rector's Log Book, at the start of the next session (1951-52) states:

> "No music teacher has yet been appointed..... The music classes were distributed among the staff but this arrangement is most unsatisfactory since not only does Music itself languish, but the morale of the school is impaired."

On 21st September, 1951, the Rector's Log Book continues:

> "No appointment has yet been made in Music. The Music classes continue to be taken for other subjects by the remainder of the staff. Information has, however, been received... that a teacher was appointed but declined to accept the appointment through lack of a house."

At last, on 31st January, 1952, the Rector's Log Book records:

> "Information has been received... that Mrs Down will commence teaching Music on Tuesday, 5th February; she will teach on Tuesdays and Thursdays. Her appointment ends a vacancy of eleven months."

Mrs Down's arrival at the school must have been most welcome. Bearing in mind the accommodation problems of that time, it is not surprising to read in the School Log Book that, from October 1953, Music was taught in the Domestic Science Room.

1954 saw the arrival of Mr Colvin Greig as teacher in charge of Music. An interesting comment in the Rector's Log Book for 24th December, 1959 states:

> "In the evening carols sung by the school choir were broadcast on VHF wavelength. A party of pupils under Mr Greig's supervision sang carols at different places in Fortrose and Rosemarkie on Monday evening. A sum of £4/4/9 which was realised was sent to the Highland Orphanage, Inverness."

At the start of the 1960's, the Principal Teacher of Music was still not full time at Fortrose. During Session 1961-62, it appears that Mr Greig was in the Academy on Monday afternoons, Tuesdays, Thursdays and Friday afternoons. Mr Greig left Fortrose in September 1963 to take up a post as assistant lecturer in Music in Aberdeen College of Education. Mrs Down agreed to take the Music classes pending the arrival of a new P.T. of Music. Mr Bevan Baker arrived at the start of the session in 1964, giving several years service to the Academy before leaving to teach at Avoch Primary School.

MISS A. FRASER

Miss Fraser, Principal Teacher of Music, remembers that, in her own schooldays, "Music" lessons were actually "singing" lessons; she certainly had no objections to this state of affairs, for she loved singing and recalls doing a great deal of singing at school. Instrumental instruction was virtually unheard of, except in the piano. Some major events of the year involved Miss Fraser in singing; school concerts — in both her Primary and Secondary days — were big affairs into which would go a great deal of pupil and staff effort. The Mod was an important national event and the Ross and Cromarty Music Festival was certainly the highlight of the year. Choirs were very plentiful in the area, and very popular in schools. No doubt many people have realised that this choral activity in schools seems to have lost its appeal for some reason and that time spent on this has greatly declined — a fact which our present P.T. of Music regrets. Perhaps the attractions of new developments in music in schools — and there are many — have been too powerful and have drawn potentially first class "choral" pupils to explore other areas.

As a pupil, Miss Fraser enjoyed all forms of musical activity. We all tend to find that if we enjoy an activity, our interest is stimulated to such an extent that no matter how hard in reality it may be, we find it easy. Her enthusiasm for music was such that it won the decision concerning which course of study Miss Fraser was to undertake on leaving school. She had considered languages, but decided to opt for Music — in spite of the lack of career guidance in the matter! Studying at Edinburgh University, she graduated Bachelor of Music, and after training as a teacher at Moray House, she began teaching at Dunfermline High School, where she was to remain for three years.

In 1988, singing is simply one of the several aspects of Music-making. There are now many more opportunities for pupil centred learning; the purchase of keyboards and headphones has allowed pupils to make their own music in a way hitherto unimagined. The developments in electronics, and the appearance of relatively cheap Japanese instruments, have been a strong factor in bringing about this change. Our Music Department's attitude is one of "All welcome"; the idea of music as something to be developed only for "good" singers and instrumentalists has long gone. Instrumental instruction in Fortrose Academy is now taken by $\frac{1}{8}$ of the school pupils. An increased number of staff means a greater variety in musical activities, and this in turn involves the Principal Teacher more deeply in a co-ordinating role, although, as Miss Fraser points out, there is still a need on occasions for the more traditional "musical director" — most obviously in the production of the school musicals. One other most beneficial change must be mentioned — the reduction in class size. In Miss Fraser's time as a pupil, the numbers in a music class could be anything from thirty to fifty! Now numbers in music classes are certainly more reasonable, allowing for individual attention for pupils, who are working at their own pace with music to match their abilities. This must surely be very much more likely to gain, for instance, some degree of "literacy" in staff notation, an achievement which was almost impossible in the "old days", unless pupils had piano lessons outside school.

80

"GUYS AND DOLLS".

CROMARTY JUNIOR SECONDARY SCHOOL
THE CLOSURE OF ITS SECONDARY DEPARTMENT, 1966.

The first entry in the Fortrose Academy Log Book for the session 1966-67 is dated 23 August, and it records a major change:

"The school re-opened today. There were present about 30 pupils who had been transferred from Cromarty J.S. School as a consequence of its closing. Five part-time teachers together with a Maths/Science teacher were added to the staff in order to cope with our increased numbers."

The 30 pupils referred to above were not the only Cromarty area pupils in Fortrose Academy: pupils who had passed the "Eleven Plus" examination had come to Fortrose for a considerable number of years. From the 1920s, pupils had been coming to Fortrose for their senior secondary education. Before that time, they had tended to go to Invergordon or Dingwall for their later years of secondary schooling, and it was no doubt the start of Neil Fraser's bus service that encouraged pupils to turn to Fortrose Academy.

That the school in Cromarty was a happy one there seems little doubt, for one teacher, arriving in 1926, actually remained there for the whole of her teaching career, leaving only when she retired in 1974! She remembers a wide variety of subjects being taught in Cromarty in the 1920s, including Navigation. (This natural interest in the sea was maintained; Cromarty was featured in "The Press and Journal" Week-end Review of 27 July, 1963 and it shows no fewer than five pictures of pupils and their activities at Cromarty J.S. School. One such photograph shows two boys at work making a boat. The Headmaster at that time was Mr John Rae, then also Vice-Commodore of the Cromarty Yacht Club).

As in Fortrose, teachers at Cromarty in the 1920s were expected to teach a number of subjects, and this long-serving member of staff thought nothing of taking 'gym' for instance. She had, I found, spent some of her earlier years as a pupil in Ullapool, one of her teachers there being Mr K. Macleod, later Rector at Fortrose Academy from 1913 to 1949.

Another retired teacher, now living in Fortrose, Mrs Fraser, also clearly remembers her days as a teacher in the secondary department at Cromarty. This post provided the start of her teaching career, and she recalls the details of her first journey to Cromarty — crossing from Invergordon in Albert Watson's launch in what must have been rather choppy conditions, for the sea spray did its best to dampen her clothes, but had no success with her enthusiasm. Arriving in 1935, Mrs Fraser, who was to spend some five years there, taught English, History, Geography and Latin. The Headmaster at that time was Mr Malcolm, who taught Maths and Science. A variety of other subjects was taught, including some by itinerant teachers.

Mrs Fraser taught in a room at the front of the school, and the layout of the desks meant that she usually faced the windows when at work, thereby being able to notice such sights as the fleet coming in. She was at first puzzled by the ability of pupils (who had their backs to the windows) to know immediately when such interesting events were happening, but was soon to realise how it was done. Thanks to the glass framing of a large picture of Hugh Miller, the pupils could see, in its reflection, anything going on outside!

It is evident that the Black Isle communities then, as now, were busily engaged in organising an active social life, and Cromarty was no exception. There existed, for instance, a thriving Literary Society, and, as the new teacher of English, Mrs Fraser was asked to address this group. Many areas too had their own badminton teams and Mrs Fraser was an enthusiastic player. In the "Ross-shire Journal" of November 19, 1982, an article dealt with the year 1938 and reported that Cromarty had defeated Conon by eight matches to nil in the first round of the Rosehaugh Badminton Cup Competition. Included in the Cromarty team were Miss Nicolson (ie. Mrs Fraser) and Mr A. Mackenzie — who was the husband of Mrs J.M. Mackenzie featured in an earlier chapter!

Week-end trips to Inverness were enjoyed and Mrs Fraser would go by the north side of the Black Isle, to Conon Bridge and then round to Inverness. Perhaps visitors to that town would call in for refreshment at one of its "Tea-rooms". The official guide to Inverness in 1933 shows a photograph of a most spacious tea-room at 46 Academy Street, called Burnett's. Other tea-rooms and hotels advertise in the guide, and their prices naturally seem attractive for us today, one major hotel advertising its High Tea, with Fish and Meat, for 3/6 and Dinner for 5/6. We must be careful however, not to be taken in by what seem to be marvellous bargains of earlier periods and bear in mind that incomes in those distant days also seem very low. Nevertheless, glancing through old guide-books is always fascinating, stirring memories of phrases now out of fashion. I can remember when Union Street in Aberdeen, in the 1950s, had several famous "Tea-Rooms". Quite suddenly, it seemed, they had all gone, to be replaced by the snack bars and fast food outlets we know today.

MRS BROWN: SCHOOL SECRETARY

Mrs Brown's family connections with this area go back some time — in fact her mother was born near Avoch and went to live in Avoch in the 1880s. Some years ago, while I was chatting to Mrs Brown about her own schooldays, I found out that we were able to discuss some shared memories — for as pupils we both attended Mackie Academy, Stonehaven! As a youngster, Mrs Brown had stayed at Glenbervie, and travelled to school at Stonehaven, by train from Drumlithie. Leslie Mitchell (or Lewis Grassic Gibbon) was at "the Mackie" at that time, being a year or two ahead of Mrs Brown. No doubt many people will remember that this famous author had his fictional characters make some choice comments about Stonehaven and its Academy! When Mrs Brown was a pupil at Mackie Academy, the Rector was a Mr Knox; he was still the Rector when I arrived in Primary 1, although he retired not long afterwards.

Mrs Brown came to Avoch in 1945. There was a field next to her home, part of her mother's property. This was the area on which, in the early 1950s, there was constructed a pond; trees were planted, and a couple of boats were brought in for anyone to use. Swans appeared too, and the scene must have been quite pleasing to the eye. The pond stayed in reasonable condition for some years, before the site deteriorated. It has now been completely redeveloped.

Mrs Brown began her association with Fortrose Academy just after the Easter holidays in 1960, when she was appointed part-time secretary, working two hours every day. The previous secretary had been Mrs Kathleen Munro, who had left for family reasons. Unfortunately, in November 1960, Mrs Brown was taken ill and was off work for three months. The post was however kept open for her and she returned to the Academy — now working three hours every day. Her work then consisted largely of typing letters, examinations etc. Accommodation during those earlier years must have been far from ideal, for she had no place of her own in the school, and had to work either in the women's staff room, or, when Mr MacPhail, the Rector, was teaching, in his office.

The School Log Book, in listing the staff at the start of the session 1962/63 notes: "Mrs Brown has now been appointed full-time clerkess." She was soon to have a car of her own and this was to prove a great help. When the new buildings opened, Mrs Brown at last was given her own office. (It is now the Depute Rector's office).

Those teachers who taught in the school in the sixties will remember that Mrs Brown came round every classroom on a Monday morning to sell the canteen-tickets. This was always efficiently done, although Mrs Brown remembers that when the change to decimal currency was made — on Monday, 15 February, 1971 — the week's ticket sales took considerably longer to administer. She was also responsible for doing "registration" — or "attendance" as it was then more commonly called; this was done both in the morning and the afternoon, with the main register being completed every day.

Mrs Brown retired at Easter, 1972, but returned for a brief period because the new secretary, Mrs S. Macdonald, was not yet free to take up duty. Mrs Brown certainly missed the company of those at Fortrose Academy, for she had especially enjoyed seeing the pupils, from the age of five, coming up through the school. Equally staff and pupils during her years as Secretary will remember Mrs Brown as a highly efficient and extremely helpful secretary. She stayed on in her Avoch home for some years, and then moved to Station Crescent in Fortrose, where she has been living for the past nine years.

THE P.T.A.

Fortrose Academy has for some years enjoyed the support of a thriving Parent — Teacher Association, which has undertaken a great deal of hard work on behalf of the school. Fortunately, the Minutes of the first formal meeting, held to get the whole idea of a P.T.A. off the ground, are still available and are now quoted extensively. The meeting was held on 9th June, 1961.

"A meeting, fairly representative of staff and parents of pupils attending the Academy was held on 9th June. Canon Dobson, who was in the Chair, explained the purpose of the meeting — to further the promotion of a P.T. Association. After a brief history of preliminary work done with a view to forming such an Association, Mr MacPhail mentioned various ways in which it could help

a) Parents:-

1). by giving them, through closer contacts with the teaching staff, a better idea of what teachers are trying to do.
2). by giving them a closer knowledge of the working of the school.
3). by giving them an opportunity to discuss changes in the school curriculum with the staff.

and b) Teachers:-

1). by enabling parents to understand what a teacher is trying to do.
2). by raising funds for the school.
3). by supporting activities of various departments in the school.

and c) The School:-

1). by giving their support to the school.
2). by giving practical help to a school for which the authorities sometimes seem remote and unpredictable.

After discussion it was unanimously agreed to form a Parent-Teacher Association."

The Minutes continue by outlining decisions concerning the draft constitution, and then details of the Office Bearers and Committee members are given:

"...... session 1961/62.

Hon. President : Mr MacPhail.
President : Miss Noble.
Vice President : Mr MacKay.
Secretary : Mrs Crawford.
Treasurer : Mr Goodall.

Members of Committee:-

Mrs Alexander   Mr Morrison
Mrs Munro   Mr Campbell
Mrs Barnes   Mr Skinner

Tea was served and an opportunity given to parents and staff to meet each other. After tea various suggestions were put forward for the consideration of the Committee when arranging a programme of activities. Eg. Talk from Careers' Officer, Films about schools, Whist Drives to raise funds for, for example, instruments for school orchestra and the publicising of functions.

Canon Dobson was thanked for so kindly chairing the meeting and Miss Munro and Miss Patience for providing tea."

The title "Honorary President" has always been held by the Rector of the time. The first President, Miss Noble, had already given many years of service to Fortrose Academy and was to retire during the following session, with, as the Rector's Log Book records, 45 years of teaching completed. Her name first appears on school staff lists for the beginning of the session in 1916. This was a difficult time for the school and Miss Noble's readiness, as a young teacher, to undertake a variety of duties can be illustrated by these extracts from the Rector's Log Book for 1917:

"January 19, 1917 : This week Miss Noble undertook to teach the Cookery Class, and her work was so successful that an attempt was made to overtake the Cookery lessons missed.....

April 27, 1917 : The Latin class of selected First Year pupils which was initiated last week has set enthusiastically to work in full swing under Miss Noble."

July 9, 1917 : ..... Miss Noble took the first year for science."

All these duties were undertaken in addition to her 'usual' work! Miss Noble was typical of a number of teachers who gave many years of service to the school. Recognition of the effort she made over those years for her pupils was clear when she was unanimously re-elected P.T.A. President (in October, 1962) for another year — the only such person, to my knowledge, to be invited to do so; her own suggestion at that meeting, that "a parent and a teacher might hold office alternately as President" has become accepted as the norm.

Since its formation, the P.T.A. has arranged many meetings on a huge variety of subjects; it has raised large amounts of money for the benefit of the pupils; it has also arranged many social functions, where parents and teachers meet informally. This last mentioned category, has without doubt, lingered long in the memories of those who attended P.T.A. Social Evenings around 1970, for it was the custom at that time for staff to take to the stage and entertain the parents. The highlight of the evening was always the "Staff Song", written by Mr A.G. Mackenzie, Depute Rector. Here is the staff ballad of (I think) Session 1969-70. It was sung to the tune "The Barnyards o' Dalgetty".

1. We're the teachers; You're the parents
   We're the folk who teach your kids
   Though to you they may be angels
   They can make us 'flip our lids'
       Chorus

2. I'm the Rector: I'm the head man
   Never common — never coarse
   When a pupil misbehaves
   I advocate the use of force.
       Chorus

3. I am one who teaches English
   Every month I'm paid by cheque
   In spite of all my airs and graces
   I know the pupils call me Eck.
       Chorus

4. I'm another English teacher
   Shakespeare, Milton — all that hash
   When the bell is rung for classes
   I'm in Room 8 like a flash.
       Chorus

5. We teach kids to be athletic
   Keep them fit with exercise,
   Make them clamber up rope ladders
   And then watch them drop like flies.
       Chorus

6. Pupils come to my Art classes
   It's a struggle to the death.
   Some can paint like Boticelli
   Some can hardly draw their breath
       Chorus

7. We teach all the younger classes
   S.R.A. and projects too.
   When the leaving age is raised
   It's Avoch for us in '72
       Chorus

8. French and German are my subjects
   Spreche Deutsch and Parlez vous
   But when I am marking papers
   Language can be pretty blue.
       Chorus

9. I teach Chemistry and Physics
   Work with solids, liquids, gas.
   I can fill the school with fumes
   And clear out every single class.
       Chorus

10. We've a technical Department
    Hammers, chisels — all that gear
    When we get a likely pupil
    We make him an engineer
        Chorus

11. Certain pupils study music
    Piano, violins and trombones
    Though I recommend Beethoven
    They prefer the Rolling Stones.
        Chorus

12. We are sharing Modern Studies
    Geography and History
    And we know what pupils call us
    I am Tufty, I'm John D.
        Chorus

13. Now that we have sung our ditty
    Tried to make you laugh and cheer.
    We wish you a Merry Christmas
    And a Very Good New Year.

OUTDOOR ACTIVITIES
1968-74

Hill-walking and orienteering are good examples of outdoor activities which have enjoyed a particular popularity in recent years. Orienteering especially is an exciting sport which now attracts a tremendous following, combining as it does the need for skilful and accurate mapwork with the necessity for speed and physical fitness.

It is a fact that Fortrose Academy was one of the schools that was early involved in orienteering, due almost completely to the interest of Mr A. MacDonald, Principal Teacher of Technical Education up to 1974. (He had first started teaching in Fortrose Academy in 1960). His work in orienteering was only part of his interest in outdoor pursuits, for he also organised hill-walking expeditions, hill-walking camps, and was an enthusiastic advocate of the Morvich

Outdoor Centre on the west coast. Mr Jock Watt was then a Principal Teacher in Invergordon and with Mr T. Strang of Plockton High School, did a great deal to encourage outdoor activities in the county.

HILL WALKING

The "School Camp" became an established feature of the school calendar, staff and pupils involved being allowed a few days off school towards the end of the summer term to enjoy the hills in some beautiful areas of the Highlands. The Rector, Mr MacPhail, was a very keen supporter of these pursuits.

The first camp, in 1968, was a back-packing trip from Achnasheen to Cluanie. Ask anyone who has been on such a trip, and all the problems of such a trip will be readily explained! Heavier items — like tents — have to be carried all the way, of course, as have other necessities, like food. The weather on the '68 trip was really too good — the sun shone brightly every day and the heat became quite oppressive. Mr MacDonald's legs suffered so much from sunburn that he could not bend them at the knees at all and had to walk the last day completely "straight-legged". One first year pupil had mistakenly thought that he needed to provide extra food and brought a number of cans of fruit etc. with him. These cans had slipped to the foot of his rucksack and were rubbing against his back. It was only on the last day that these surplus tins were discovered, by which time the pupil's back was quite bruised! Midges were a particular nuisance, forcing pupils up at 3am; one pupil's eyes were so swollen that they appeared to be almost shut. It must have been with some relief that these courageous hill-walkers returned to school — where they immediately had to change and take their places on stage, for the seniors in the group were part of the choir at the Music Festival, held that year in Fortrose.

These hill-walking camps brought together junior and senior pupils and indeed witnessed a form of liaison between Fortrose Academy and Avoch Junior Secondary School, for, as the picture here shows, pupils from both schools might well join the camp. Four pupils are from Fortrose Academy and four from Avoch Junior Secondary School.

Normally four tents were used, provided by the County, as were additional items of equipment like rucksacks, cagoules and some utensils for cooking.

I myself joined the staff of Fortrose Academy in 1969 and enjoyed the 1970 camp at Strathconon, where the weather was at times very wet. Nevertheless, pupils "on duty" prepared our meals in spite of wind and rain. Here it must be admitted that Mrs J. MacDonald had always prepared our first meal, so that all we had to do was to heat the food — a very important bonus when, perhaps in poor weather, we were all busily concerned with getting our tents up! Food was always welcome; not one crumb was ever wasted on any of the school camps. It was at this 1970 camp that our pupils, ever resourceful, decided to use a small stream as a refrigerator, in which to place packets of milk; unfortunately, the first night saw heavy rain which turned the stream into a fast flowing torrent, which carried away most of the milk. Not to be beaten, the boys, on the following morning, searched downstream, and recovered the milk packets undamaged!

This camp was at West Glen Orrin in 1969. The pupils are, left to right: Back row, standing: T. Macdonald; A. MacPherson; P. McDonald; G. Oman. Front row: B. Macgregor; F. Clark; S. Sharp; R. Shanks. Teacher: Mr A. Morrison, P.T. of P.E. Mr A. MacDonald took the picture.

All camps were enjoyable, whatever the weather. The sunny clear days were, of course, a delight, when exertion in reaching the top of a pass or mountain was further rewarded by a beautiful view. (One pupil, never one to be impressed by anything, would actually produce a pack of cards and try to get a game started, while others were entranced by their surroundings).

This picture shows how enjoyable the conditions could be. It was taken on the high ground at the west end of Corrie Lair, when the pupils were on their way up to Beinn Liath Mhor. The teacher on the right is a very young-looking Mr J.D. Campbell. (Page 90).

It might occasionally happen that our campsite would be near some useful permanent shelter. This proved most welcome one year when we arrived at our selected site in the most appalling weather. We were fortunate in having a shooting "bothy" beside our camp-site, at the west end of Loch Fannich, and it was not long before we were comfortably settled in. This bothy apparently 'enjoyed' a reputation for close encounters of the ghostly kind! We had been

assured that, only a short time previously, a party of H.M. forces' personnel had left the bothy in the middle of the night, terrified by some strange happenings. Imagine my feelings that first evening, when, looking out a window, I saw one of our pupils (who had gone outside to attend a call of nature) running back through the thick mist pursued by a strange large mysterious white mass! I rushed to the door, our brave pupil thankfully stepped inside, and only then did I realise that the alarm had been caused by nothing more frightening than a pure white, and rather inquisitive, Highland pony — one of several we later saw in the area.

1974 saw the last camp organised by Mr A MacDonald, before he left to teach in Inverness. This camp was in the Glencarron mountains, and our camp-site one of the most ideal we had ever found. Situated beside the Allt a' Chonais, which at that point was deep enough for swimming, we pitched camp on an area of grass that almost resembled a well cared for lawn!

Here are the pupils present on this camp, photographed half-way up Sgurr nan Ceannaichen. Mr MacDonald can be seen third from the left.

At this time — June 1974 — the school did not have its own minibus and hired buses of various sizes from Mr Robert Macrae, Fortrose, who always proved most helpful.

ORIENTEERING

If hill-walking and camping were summer-season activities, orienteering was given its place in the winter months. Many pupils interested in hill-walking were, naturally enough, keen to take part in orienteering, and thereby extend their navigational skills for use in the mountains.

Towards the end of October, a start would be made to introduce younger pupils to the apparent mysteries of orienteering! Lunch-time classes would be held to instruct pupils in the use of maps and Silva compasses, and simple exercises on the use of these vital items would be arranged in the areas around the school. After this course in basics, pupils would then get the chance to try out the real thing — usually on a Saturday morning in an area familiar to most — the Hill of Fortrose being very useful on such occasions. Many pupils enjoyed orienteering outings in Shantullich Woods, near Munlochy, or at Ord Hill, North Kessock, two of several areas for which Mr MacDonald had not only prepared very detailed maps, but courses of varying difficulty to suit all pupils.

Pupils welcomed the chance to test their orienteering abilities in areas less familiar to them. This meant that pupils had to go further afield, which in turn involved longer outings, with their attendant vital needs — eg food — and hot food at that, since pupils would be outside in, perhaps, cold weather. In this connection, one orienteering outing at Fairburn provided a good instance of support from the local community. On this occasion our pupils enjoyed hot food, thanks to a retired couple who agreed to heat up sausage rolls and pies and see that there was plenty refreshingly hot tea. They were in fact Mr and Mrs Maclean. Mrs Maclean was a Londoner; Mr Maclean had been born and brought up in the Fairburn area, but had gone south to spend his working life in London. They decided on retiral, to come to Fairburn.

At inter-school orienteering events, food was always provided as part of the organisation of the day. Day trips were made as far as Ardgour, and the standard of organisation was always high, taking into account many factors besides food. The safety of pupils was always a priority. Pupils from their early lunch-time meetings at Fortrose were instructed in the use of safety bearings to bring them out of trouble in a given area; perhaps just as well, too, for at one meeting at Fort William, the high ground on which the orienteers were competing completely disappeared in a sudden snowstorm. The organisers of that particular event were certainly taking no chances, for they had ensured the presence of many radio-equipped soldiers across the whole area.

Many orienteering outings were undertaken to areas which were a considerable distance from the school, some involving overnight stops. Mr A. MacDonald remembers that, when attending competitions in the south of Scotland, in the late 1960s, it took at least 5 hours to get to Edinburgh by car — and longer if a bus was used. The completion of the 'new' A9 was still some way off. The trips to take part in the Scottish Championships were normally made in February too, and the orienteers could never be quite sure if the roads would be clear for the return journey. Probably the most distant trip was to the Border country, to Innerleithen, to take part in a Scottish Schools competition. I remember that we stayed overnight at a Sports Centre in Leith, beds being either thick rubber mats on the floor, or several chairs placed in line! Nonetheless, the pupils slept soundly that night, for their evening had been spent in taking on teams of Leith teenagers in a variety of sports available at the Centre.

A number of orienteering days were arranged at Morvich, where the Authority had an outdoor centre which schools could reserve for their use. The photograph over shows pupils about to start an orienteering exercise at Dorisduain Woods, which are near the Morvich Centre. Fortrose Academy's Physical Education teachers were always most supportive, and the picture shows Miss Tuach, second from the right. The date was 17th February, 1973, and we

had arrived just after a heavy snowfall. Fortunately the weather then remained sunny and dry and the outing proved most enjoyable; the competitively minded orienteers eagerly accepted the extra challenge of the deep snow, while the "We're out to enjoy ourselves" pupils rightly found extra diversions on their way; one of our slides shows a beautifully made snowman on one of the pupil's routes. Clearly some pupils had not been too concerned about getting their course completed in record time!

The Morvich Outdoor Centre was used on many occasions by Fortrose Academy in the period up to 1975, for a variety of activities, not necessarily always hill-walking, for the Centre is in an area of considerable interest for a variety of school subjects — notably History. The outings developed a most valuable form of education outwith the usual classroom situation and provided pupils with the chance to work together and undertake responsibilities and tasks which they themselves had to organise. These duties which included basics like the preparation and serving of meals, the making of packed lunches, washing-up and cleaning the Centre, were done with remarkable efficiency. Keeping expenses of Morvich visits to a minimum was important, and great care was taken to stock up with good quality supplies at the most competitive prices. Before any camps and Morvich visits, Mrs J. MacDonald would plan a major expedition to buy in supplies, with all items bought, from a variety of sources, at the best possible bargain prices.

In 1973-74, there were three first year visits, each department in the school contributing work for the pupils to complete at Morvich. The mornings and afternoons were spent outside, the evenings being normally set aside for school work of the classroom kind. Pupils carried out this evening work session with surprising readiness — on one occasion, after 10pm, when the pupils were doing Algebra, one teacher had to ask: "Don't you think you should finish?" There were entertainments laid on too! Impromptu concerts and dancing sessions were popular, and although there were films, no one wanted to watch them. There was no television.

At one time, it was hoped that all first year pupils would have the opportunity to spend a week at Morvich — such outings being spread over the session, of course, since the centre could take only so many pupils at one time. It was thought, however, that this would be an interruption too serious in the normal classwork of the pupils and the idea was dropped.

MRS C. BASSINDALE
CLASS OF '71!

This photograph of class IIA was taken during Session 1970-71

Mrs Catriona Bassindale was a pupil in that class and can be seen in the back row, first on the left. She most kindly agreed to provide some written comments on her days in the Academy — from a pupil's point of view!

The pupils in the picture are: (Left to right)

BACK ROW: Catriona Armstrong; Frances Noon; Ian Ross; Thomas McPhee; Anne MacIntosh; Fiona Moyes; Shirley McIntosh.

MIDDLE ROW: Kay Fraser; Thelma Logan; John Ross; Stuart Davis; David Drummond; Allan Gilbert; Marion Eastwood; Julia Ellery; Ian Reid.

FRONT ROW: Hilda Storm; Billy Winton; Alastair Mackenzie; Stewart Huntly; John McEwan; Bruce Morrison; Colin Campbell; Douglas Middleton; Jane Anderson.

Mrs Bassindale writes:

"I joined Fortrose Academy in July, 1970, after moving to Scotland from the south of England. I was in the second year, which was divided into two classes — 2A and 2 Alpha. Naturally I felt strange at first, especially as everyone already knew one another from the first year. However, it didn't take long to get to know the teachers and the school routine.

I remember our English teacher, Mr Mackenzie, well as there was always a lot of humour in his class. He also had a passion for singing, and we were often treated to a song during the lesson. Mr MacPhail was Rector for my first year at the Academy. When he retired he was replaced by Mr Macleod. For me, Mr Macleod seemed easily approachable as I had known him as a teacher the year before. When I reached third year, decisions had to be made about subjects for "O" grade. I decided on History, Modern Studies, French, Biology and compulsory English, Maths and Arithmetic. "O" Grades were taken in the Town Hall, Fortrose. However, when I took Highers, the school gym was used. In the fifth year I took up Secretarial Studies and went on to take an SHND in Secretarial at College, finding the start in shorthand and typing most valuable.

In my third year at school I went on a school cruise on the S.S. Uganda. I have mixed memories of the trip. On the one hand, I remember the awful food and often feeling sea-sick; on the other, visiting many interesting places in the Baltic more than compensated for the discomforts on the ship.

School parties were an annual event not to be missed. First, however, a few weeks of dancing had to be undertaken during P.E. classes. These were awesome occasions for both boys and girls, who took up position on either side of the gym only pairing up when absolutely necessary. I often seemed to be left unattached or with the boy who had the most severe case of "two left feet". In spite of all this, the parties were well attended and enjoyed.

The only activities that I was ever involved in out of school hours were netball and hockey matches against other schools in the area. Discipline in the school must have been good as I really do not remember any use of the belt, although a few teachers did possess one. Prefects were known to give out lines as a punishment, and any serious offence was dealt with by the Rector.

When I look back on my days at Fortrose Academy most memories are good. I think everyone tends to forget the bad memories, and I really cannot think of what I liked least about my days at school. I think that the year I spent in sixth year was my happiest as you were given some responsibility. Also many of the friends I made in the school are still friends today, and we can all clearly remember our days at the Academy."

Here is the Bassindale family in 1987. Mr Bassindale is also a former pupil of Fortrose Academy. Their three daughters are, from the left, Amy, Sophie and Gemma.

THE FAIRY GLEN BRIDGE PROJECT
SESSION 1972-73

THOSE INVOLVED:

STAFF: Mr A. MacDonald, Team Co-ordinator; Mr Neil Grant; Miss A. Sanderson; Mr J. Brough; Miss P. Stewart; Mr J.D. Campbell.

PUPILS:

Kathleen Anderson	Irene Cameron	Lorna Gilbert
Shiona MacKay	Marion Morrison	Flora Reid
Donald Mackay	Donald MacKenzie	John Ross
Graeme Geddes	Colin Gill	David Innes
Roderick MacDonald	Allan MacIntosh	Colin MacKay
David MacKenzie	Alexander Maclean	David Williamson

AT WORK ON THE BRIDGE

This was an interesting, and successful, attempt to make a break from the normal arrangements of timetabling and staffing in order to establish a form of team-teaching with one particular class. It was agreed that this class would undertake a special study of one topic, and that the pupils would be involved in a fair amount of practical work. The Rector, Mr D.W. Macleod, had already welcomed the idea and had constructed the session's timetable with this project in mind. Accordingly, a fourth year class, not involved on that morning in any 'O' Grade work, was timetabled to spend Friday, from 9.15 am to noon, on this study. Further, it was arranged that there would always be two or three members of the teachers' team available at any given time during Friday mornings, so that the class could be split up to work on different aspects of the topic: one teacher might be working with the group from 9.15 to the interval, another might be on duty for the first period and then from the interval until noon. Certainly, most teachers were with the group for at least two hours. In addition to all these arrangements, there were, for most of Friday mornings, always at least two rooms available for use by the group.

It had been decided that the group would make a detailed study of BRIDGES. The reasons for the choice were many, but foremost among them were the facts that improvements in communications have always been of immense importance to the Highlands, that such a study would give enormous scope for pupils' practical work, and, of course, that the early 1970s saw much discussion about the possible bridging of the Moray and Cromarty Firths.

The school did not have a minibus in 1972, and so teachers' cars were occasionally used to transport pupils around the area; on one or two outings a bus was hired to allow the whole group of pupils and staff to visit certain areas. A considerable number of bridges was studied and details noted about types of construction, materials used, age, adequacy of the bridge (at its time of building and in the 1970s), any interesting features, approaches and so on. A large collection of slides of bridges was built up over the session and these were useful to illustrate features of bridges which were too far away for a class visit. Pupils were involved in various investigations, including the compilation of traffic census returns on different roads, and the conduct of interviews with motorists on the Kessock Ferry. A survey was carried out, local residents being asked their opinions on how the Kessock Bridge would affect local shopping habits.

The Kessock Ferry.

Although the pupils were busily at work in carrying out their own research in a number of directions, it had been decided that one major exercise would be undertaken — involving all the pupils in the group. This was to be the construction of a bridge by the pupils themselves. In fact, not only were the pupils to build the bridge, but also to arrange some way of their own to provide the finance for the materials used in its construction.

It goes without saying that neither staff nor pupils of Fortrose Academy can just go and build a bridge wheresoever they choose. With the full support of local councillors, including Provost Alexander and Town Clerk Mr Lackie, it was decided that the bridge would be constructed across the Fairy Glen burn, at a particular point not far from the lower waterfall. While referring to Mr Alexander and Mr Lackie, it should be remembered that their sons had been pupils at Fortrose Academy; David Lackie had been involved in an earlier community venture, when pupils of the Technical Education Department made a plaque for the Brahan Seer's Stone at Chanonry Point.

The construction of the bridge meant a great deal of work for the pupils, for the materials used were heavy. The immediate area too had to be cleared, and stepped approaches to the bridge prepared.

Pupils enjoying a moment's rest before starting the morning's work.

The stone foundations were built up first, followed by the main supports. The walk-way cross-pieces were put in place, and hand-rails installed. The actual building of the bridge took in the region of 6 to 8 weeks. Remembering that all the work had to be done on Friday mornings, and that materials had to be prepared and taken to the site, plus the fact that pupils of course had actually to get there and back in the given time, it must be said that the pupils carried out the work with considerable efficiency.

The financial side of the project was tackled with equal vigour! A number of pupils worked on the preparation and publication of a Cookery Book. Pupils visited friends, neighbours and other residents in their home areas and invited them to hand in their favourite recipes. A week or two later, there were all sorts of interesting cookery ideas coming in from all areas — even ones far distant from the Black Isle. Recipes were studied, chosen and arranged in different categories. Mrs Brown, who had retired from her post as school secretary at the end of the previous school session, gave valuable help in the typing of stencils; Mr A.G. Mackenzie had been asked to suggest a heading or title for the book — and very speedily came forward with several. Francesca MacIntyre designed the cover, and before long "WHAT'S COOKIN'?" was on sale to the public. Many copies were sold, and sufficient capital raised to cover the costs of bridge-building. Members of the teaching team of course enjoyed taking part in bridge-building and cookery book composition. Miss A. Sanderson is shown in the picture overleaf.

Many people will no doubt remember the sunny evening of 19th June, 1973, for it marked the climax of the group's work — the official opening of the bridge. Parents, staff, members of the Town Council, pupils in the group, and other friends walked along the Fairy Glen path towards the new bridge. The attitude of keen support from our local councillors was clearly shown by the example of Dean of Guild Mr John Mackay; although walking was difficult because of arthritic troubles, he was determined to be there, and had set off an hour early to be at the bridge on time. A stop was made about half-way to carry out some tree-planting; Mr Forsyth

had seen to the provision of the young trees and tools with which to plant them. He had also been of great help in providing the right materials for the bridge.

At the bridge itself, there were no speeches; Mrs Brown cut the tape to mark the official opening, and one of our pupils, Flora Reid, performed the role of piper for the ceremony.

After the Fairy Glen ceremony, everybody returned to the school assembly hall, where the pupils took to the stage to explain different aspects of the year's work. A tape-slide sequence on bridges had been prepared by pupils and this too was shown. Mr D.W. Macleod offered the bridge to the community and Provost Alexander accepted it, presenting a cheque to the school. In addition to its educational value, the project was a financial success too! Everyone particularly enjoyed the refreshment buffet, which provided a marvellous selection of different kinds of savouries, sandwiches, cakes and biscuits — all prepared by the pupils with remarkable skill. The punch (non-alcoholic) proved most popular — not a drop was left. As a result of their work over the year, the pupils involved were awarded a major school prize for their contribution to the activities of school and community.

A photograph taken just after the official opening.

This picture shows the Rector, with Provost Alexander, Mrs Brown, and Mr A. MacDonald. They are pictured in front of the plaque, in the school, on which are inscribed the names of the Rectors of the school. This plaque had been formally unveiled, at 12 noon, on Monday, 20th June, 1955, as part of the quincentenary celebrations of the Royal Burgh.

Fortrose Academy Staff. Session 1973-74
From the left:
Back row: *Mr W.R. Campbell; Mr Stout; Mr MacKinnon; Mr J.D. Campbell; Mr Patience; Mr A. MacDonald; Mr J. Sutherland; Mr Fraser; Mr Logan; Mr McCuish; Mr Brough.*
Middle row: *Miss Tuach; Mrs Benzie; Mrs Clement; Miss Macleod; Miss Fraser; Mr Webster; Mr Grant; Mrs K. Munro; Miss Sanderson; Mrs MacAdam; Miss Stewart.*
Front row: *Miss Mackay; Miss Urquhart; Mr Tait; Mrs S. Munro; Mr Mackenzie; Mr D.W. Macleod; Mr Maxwell; Mrs Holm; Mr MacIntyre; Mrs Newell.*

101

EXTRACTS FROM
A TEACHER'S DIARY....

Do you keep a diary? Some pupils — although not very many — do keep diaries, and it is not surprising that a History teacher should keep such a record of events. Here are a few extracts from my own diary, chosen for the most part, because they illustrate some important date in connection with the school.

Extracts from the diary are given first — anything in brackets which follows is merely an additional explanation where needed!

21 April, 1970 : Attended meeting at Newhall Primary School to discuss the setting up of a committee to consider the possible purchase of a training swimming pool.

(This was to be the first of many meetings of "BISPA" — the "Black Isle Swimming Pool Association". Mr Jagger and I represented Fortrose Academy PTA at these meetings. A number of fund raising events were organised and Fortrose Academy PTA donated, if I remember correctly, £100. Unfortunately, the inflation of the following years effectively brought the scheme to a standstill).

29 April, 1970 : Received first monthly cheque of over £100. It is actually £100/11/11 — after all deductions!

13 June, 1970 : The P.T.A. Sale went very well and raised £158.

22 June, 1972 : Presentation Dinner was held in the hotel here in honour of our Rector Mr MacPhail, who is retiring at the end of this session. The evening was most enjoyable. After the dinner, several teachers or husbands/wives of teachers entertained the company to stories and songs. It was interesting to see some former teachers of whom I had heard a great deal but never met.
Four other members of staff are also leaving the school at the end of this session.

20 August, 1973: Started the session in a new room — Room 30. The Primary Department had used this new building for a short period at the end of last session.
There is a staff-room in this building, and so teachers here will not have to cross the quadrangle to go to the main staff-room at intervals.
(The new building referred to here is the block which runs parallel to the Greengates.)

12 Feb., 1974 : Petrol now costing 50p a gallon!

3 Oct., 1975 : No L.T.A. — normal classes instead.
(This was the only Friday afternoon since L.T.A. had been introduced, when "normal" classes were run. Leisure Time Activities were withdrawn for one week because of vandalism in the school grounds).

1 April, 1976 : At school in evening to see "Arsenic and Old Lace", put on by pupils under the direction of Mrs Holm.
A most entertaining performance.

From the left: *Barbara Rieder; Robin Kennedy; Isabel Munro.*

25 May, 1977 : Pupils were allowed home early today because of a grenade in the school grounds.
(A pupil from Cromarty had actually found a hand grenade in the outskirts of Fortrose, in an area which was being prepared for house-building. Taking it to school, he showed it to a teacher, who immediately saw that it was taken outside. It was placed in the hollow at the foot of the flagpole! The bomb disposal team was called and the area sealed off. Teachers however, were not allowed home. Fortunately, as it turned out, the grenade contained no explosives).

14 Nov., 1978 : Very strong winds today! In Room 30, I happened to be looking out towards Rosemarkie when I saw a great deal of our building's roof blown off; some of the heavier material landed at the side of the building, or in the Greengates area, while the lighter fabric disappeared in the Rosemarkie direction.

15 Nov., 1978 : Heavy rainfall. Rain was pouring into Room 30 today. I re-arranged desks and chairs to miss most of the water; buckets have been placed at suitable points. Plastic sacks have been bought and are to be used to protect books, jotters etc. from the wet. I hope the roof is repaired as quickly as possible!

2 March, 1979 : Today marked the end of our staff sponsored slim. For the last six weeks, I have not eaten any bread, crisps, sweets, chocolate biscuits, chips etc. The sponsored slim ended at 1pm. After the weigh-in, I enjoyed a lunch with an extra large portion of chips. After 4pm., I bought 1lb. box of Cadbury's Milk Tray.

28 Oct., 1981 : Over to a new system at the school canteen — staff and pupils now pay for the dishes etc. they choose. The "Traditional" meal is still served if pupils choose to take it, but there is a good selection of other main courses etc.

13 Jan., 1982 : A thaw is at last setting in after weeks of freezing cold weather — definitely the longest, coldest spell I have known.

2 April, 1982 : Staff/pupil hockey match did not start on time today because a helicopter of the Royal Flight landed in the King George V playing field. It is making a preparatory trip for Prince Charles' forthcoming visit to Rosemarkie.

18 May, 1982 : A decision was taken by teachers today that there be a "No Smoking" rule at staff meetings.

A staff football team, Session 1972-73.
Back row, from the left: *Mr J.D. Campbell; Mr Patience; Mr Maxwell; Mr MacKinnon; Mr Bevan Baker; Mr Brough; Mr J. Sutherland.* Front row: *Mrs S. MacDonald, School Secretary; Mr Stout; Miss Tuach; Miss Smith; Mr N. Grant; Miss Patience.*

MR D.W. MACLEOD
RECTOR: 1972 - 1986

That this chapter is concerned primarily with the years 1972 - 1986, when Mr Macleod was Rector, must not lead us to forget that those fourteen years account for less than half Mr Macleod's time at Fortrose Academy, for he had joined the staff in 1952. He was to become Rector twenty years later!

When Mr Macleod came to Fortrose Academy in 1952, he was an addition to the staff — not a replacement for a teacher who had left, and his arrival meant that there were now six full time members of staff in the secondary department. Mr MacPhail was Rector then and took his share of teaching, notably Latin; Miss Bowie (English) and Miss Barron (Maths) were the only women teaching in the Secondary Department. Mr Goodall taught Science and Mr McAdam, French. Other teachers visited the school to teach a number of subjects — P.E., Art, Technical Subjects, Needlework and Cookery. Mr Macleod was to undertake the teaching of a variety of subjects over the years — not only Geography and History, but English, some Mathematics and Religious Instruction.

When the young Mr D.W. Macleod arrived here in 1952, accommodation in the school was clearly most severely stretched; he had no room of his own and taught wherever there was space available at the time. If we think we have accommodation problems today, they must be relatively minor in contrast to the 1950s! I certainly have not yet been obliged to teach History in the canteen, nor have I had to tackle the problems of Parliamentary Reform in the woodwork room. Mr Macleod would have thought nothing of teaching History — as he did — in those areas for he was accustomed to space even less satisfactory; he could have been seen in the 1950s taking a class in the corridor, with a mobile blackboard probably his only visual aid. Even the Rector, Mr MacPhail, might be seen occasionally teaching his class in the corridor —hard times indeed!

In those far-off days of the early fifties, there were many ways in which life was rather harsh for the Academy's staff. In recent years, parking space could be very difficult to find (up to November, 1987, when new staff parking space became available) with cars of necessity being parked on the road, the existing car parks having no free bays. There were no such parking difficulties in 1952, for there were no cars parked at the school! Mr D.W. Macleod then lived at Inverness and travelled to Fortrose, via the ferry, on a James motorcycle; this make was a popular one in the 1950s and with a Villiers 98cc engine was most certainly not a fast machine. Journeys to school in winter could have been very cold, and Mr Macleod had to be well clad. Journeys must have been, in icy and snowy conditions, extremely dangerous into the bargain. He was later to get the occasional use of the family car — a 1939 Morris Series M. Drivers entering the school grounds would come in at the main gate — on the corner of Deans Road and Academy Street. Certainly for most of the 1950s, there were not many "staff" cars.

When I arrived to take charge of the History Department in 1969, I remember being introduced to Mr Macleod, who had for some time been responsible for the organisation of the Geography Department. He was a most helpful colleague, on whom I, as a newcomer to the school, could rely for sound advice.

I remember clearly the actual moment when I was told that Mr Macleod was to be our new Rector. He was actually appointed on 6th March, 1972; it was the following morning when I had arrived before 9am, and was walking along the passageway to the staffroom, that another member of staff, coming out, stopped to tell me the news. Mr Macleod was already in the

Mr and Mrs Grant and family, pictured during a visit to Fortrose in 1987.

This picture shows two members of staff: Mr Bevan Baker, P.T. of Music, and Mr J. Sutherland, P.T. of Physical Education. The pupil cheerfully looking in the direction of the camera is Fiona Hamilton, now Mrs MacDonald.

staffroom when I entered to congratulate him on his success. Some might argue that it is always very difficult for a class teacher to become the Rector of the school in which he has taught and that other teachers might find it a situation difficult to accept. This was never the case in 1972. Mr Macleod was to find that having taught in the school was a great advantage, for he was able to plan ahead for the following session, when he would actually take over as Rector.

The 1972/73 Session opened for staff on 24th August. The Rector's Log Book notes:

> "Pupils will not return until 1st September because of the raising of the school-leaving age to 16, which is effective from that date."

The Log Book records the school roll as having 153 pupils in the Primary and 287 in the Secondary Departments. There were also some new faces on the staff, including the new Principal Teacher of Geography, Mr Neil Grant, who had arrived to take over the job that Mr Macleod had done for so many years. Mr Grant carried out his new responsibilities most successfully; his active interest in sport, especially football, was to be a great asset to the school.

Pupils on their way towards Avoch by the Insh Road. The return to Fortrose was by the route of the former railway line.

106

There were many happy faces at that first staff meeting of the session on 24th August, 1972, for we heard that "lines" were to be abolished. This term referred to the practice of pupils lining up in their various year groups before going to their classes, (or assembly), at 9am, the end of the morning interval and the end of the lunch hour. Boys lined up outside the main front entrance, the girls taking up their position in the quadrangle on the other side of the school. Teachers had not cared too much for "Lines Duty", which they had normally undertaken for a month at a time; it had been even worse in wet weather, when all the pupils had to line up inside the main entrance hall area. The task of lining up all the pupils in a confined area was not always easy. Staff members were also pleased to hear that the lengths of the morning interval and the lunch-hour were to be extended.

Yet another change introduced at this time by our new Rector was the start of L.T.A. — Leisure Time Activities. We had known about this for some time of course for L.T.A. had been at the centre of a great deal of thought. The Rector himself, along with Mr J. Stout and Mr Maxwell, had put a great deal of effort into planning the new scheme. The timetable had to be changed to meet its needs, and there was extensive consultation with all staff — for all teachers were to be involved. Teachers were asked which activity they would like to offer pupils, and the pupils were then given a list from which to make their choice. It had been decided that a whole afternoon would be devoted to L.T.A. and that the day would be Friday. These basic decisions have not been changed. (By March, 1988.) Teachers who so wished could depart from their normal subject disciplines; others could develop areas connected with their subjects if they preferred. Certainly Fortrose Academy tackled L.T.A. most successfully, far more so than some other schools, where the experiment apparently proved nothing like as successful. A levy was used to bring in money, and parents expressed their approval of the scheme. Other money-raising methods were organised too; early in 1973, a sponsored walk was organised to raise funds and the two photographs were taken during that outing.

It must be admitted that one parent expressed to Mr Macleod disapproval of the whole idea. That parent was later to return to say how successful the L.T.A. had proved — a most fair minded comment. There was always a wide choice of activities offered to pupils. Here is a list of L.T.A. activities which were available during the period October to December, 1987. Although only the main headings are given here, an account of all activities is provided to help pupils in their choice.

1. Cookery
2. Musical for Christmas/ Costume Making.
3. Documentary Video and Photography.
4. Woodcarving.
5. Game and Picture Making.
6. Board Games.
7. Community Involvement.
8. Scientific Pursuits and Investigations.
9. Computing Projects.
10. Swimming.
11. Cooking the Books.
12. School Newspaper.
13. Golf
14. Tapestry.
15. Football.
16. Squash.
17. Rambling.
18. Birdwatching.
19. Cycling.
20. Redwing Cruising/Sailing Maintenance.
21. Snooker/Darts.
22. Table Tennis.
23. Basketball.
24. Badminton.
25. More Dash than Cash.
26. Scottish Country Dancing.
27. Knitting and Soft Toy Making.
28. Schools Traffic Education Programme.
29. Target Shooting.
30. Outdoor Games.
31. Girls Football.

PEOPLE'S Journal

INVERNESS AND NORTHERN COUNTIES

No. 6091   Saturday, October 5, 1974.   Price 4p

COLOUR TV IN WESTER ROSS SCHOOLS

—by courtesy of Fortrose Academy

IN an unusual exercise in communications, Fortrose Academy have started a project in which educational and topical colour TV programmes are "taped" at the academy for later showing at schools in parts of the county where there is no colour TV service.

The recordings are made by videotape machines which transfer the TV programmes on to tape.

Fortrose Academy started recording programmes for its own use nearly two years ago.

Some months ago, with encouragement from Mr Ian MacNab, the county's director of education, it began passing on its recordings to other schools in the county.

At present all Ross's secondary schools and most of its major primary schools, are equipped with colour TV sets.

These, even in areas outside normal U.H.F. colour transmission range, can be linked up to playback machines which show the programmes exactly as transmitted.

Fortrose now provides the service for about 2500 pupils in Nicolson Institute, Stornoway; Plockton High School; Achtercairn J.S. School, Gairloch, and Ullapool J.S. School, as well as Avoch School, Fortrose Academy's primary feeder school, and for academy pupils themselves.

Big job

Operating the system part-time is Mrs Eleanor Macadam, of Redcraig Mill, Rosemarkie, a former Fortrose Academy physical education teacher.

As the service has extended Mrs Macadam has found her job has become more and more demanding and nearer to a full-time post.

Not only has she to record, but she has also to cope with orders from other schools. She frequently has to come in after school hours to capture programmes of topical interest.

Although all of her imposing barrage of machines can be pre-set to record at a particular time, both she and academy rector, Mr Donald Macleod, consider it important to monitor all programmes.

Unique?

The education authority have come to an arrangement with the broadcasting authorities and they are allowed to record these programmes for use exclusively in schools.

"This must be unique in Scotland," commented Mr Macleod. "Of course we have a need in Ross-shire for this service that few other counties have.

"It takes a good deal of organisation but it completely overcomes the county's geographical difficulties.

"At present we lack the staff to give a completely comprehensive service although all departments in this school make use of it and all teachers know how to operate the playback machine."

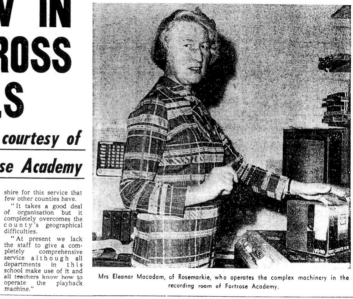

Mrs Eleanor Macadam, of Rosemarkie, who operates the complex machinery in the recording room of Fortrose Academy.

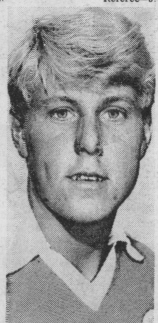

■ **THE men who mattered yesterday—OWEN COYLE (Clydebank—left), KENNY MacDONALD (Airdrie—centre), and ROSS JACK (Dunfermline—right).**

66th.

"In the Order of Merit I'm down at 129 with £7514. Every penny counts and I reckon I'll need to make another £3500 to keep my card for next year.

"I really need to have at least one more good tournament.

"My swing is sound and I've got three weeks to put in some hard graft before my next important date.

"The German Masters has a limited field and I don't rate my chances of a place too highly. Luckily, it coincides with the Scottish at Haggs Castle."

Still only 26, Steve has a great background for top class golf. A Scottish amateur cap in 1983, he lifted the Lytham Trophy, two shots ahead of a certain Charles Green Esquire.

Last year he hit the jackpot with a win in the Sunderland Open at Drumpellier, and another fine finish at the Northern Open where he finished ninth.

trophy, the
ost Angler of
ceive a cheque
unner-up gets
cially-engraved
s trophy. Third
.

e two further
thness Glass
bottles of 100
Whisky.

f the competi-
e-up of anglers
ced shortly.

STAYING
THE SWI

In the big league he tied for 22nd in the PGA Championship at Wentworth, and ended up with a cheque for £2400.

Steve knows that only that sort of form will be good enough if he is to survive the toughest fight of his life.

■ AWAY BACK on January 18, 1959, I wrote, "The infamous British weather could prove the Walker Cup Americans' best friend.

"In accepting a date in mid-May at Muirfield, the R & A

could have giv
two-hole start.

"Our boys c
be in the groove
season.

"What a dif
match could be
gust or Septen
men are in ful

Just the othe
A announced, '
Walker Cup wi
September, fol
week by the A
pionship.'

Better late t

Many regard the school's Tannoy system as an idea introduced by Mr Macleod in 1972 —incorrectly as it happens. Mr Macleod had actually set up a public address system, which could transmit radio as well, in the old buildings — long before the new additions appeared in the mid sixties. When these new buildings did appear, a Tannoy system was actually included. It operated for a short period, but then failed. It was not until Mr Macleod became Rector that the faults were located and repaired, so that the Tannoy was in fact re-introduced in 1972! And the "traffic lights" at the Rector's door? They appeared before long, installed by Mr Macleod himself, the "answer" button being on the desk.

I remember clearly the day on which the very first of the school's video cassette recorders arrived. I happened to be passing the Rector's office, and looking in, saw the Rector setting up the equipment. Along with some other teachers, I went in to examine this new machine and remember thinking how clearly it reproduced that part of a programme we had just recorded. Fortrose Academy was in fact the first school in the Highlands to have "video" and was to be the centre from which programmes were recorded and sent to other schools. Mrs Macadam was our member of staff first responsible for this duty, which was always most efficiently done; her work was much appreciated. Mrs Macadam was of course well known in the school for she had taught many years in the P.E. Department; she resigned from this P.E. post at the end of the session in 1972. The "People's Journal" of October 5th, 1974, featured the schools video recording service in a most interesting article. The account appeared on the front page and included a photograph of Mrs Macadam. I am most grateful to the editorial staff of the "People's Journal" for permission to include the article, which is shown opposite/overleaf.

The years of Mr D.W. Macleod's Rectorship saw the introduction of several new subjects; indeed, whole new departments appeared. One such was a Business Studies Department, for which Mr Macleod made plans in his first session as Rector; he invited Mr Duncan H.M.I. to the school to discuss the setting up of this proposed new department, and the visit took place on 28th November, 1972. Mr Macleod himself actually went to Glasgow to visit various schools to see how different Business Studies Departments were organised. On 13th April, 1973, he attended an interview in Dingwall at which Miss J.P. Johnston was appointed teacher of Business Studies; she took up duty at the start of the 1973/74 session. About a month before the beginning of that school year, Miss Johnston had been married, and she joined the staff as Mrs Clement. Still a probationer, the post must have presented our new teacher with a considerable challenge, having as she did not only responsibility for the department, but the additional concern that it should get off to a successful start. That it did, there is no doubt, and the new department was to play a most valuable part in the education of our pupils. The present P.T. of Business Studies is Mr L. Murdoch, who was appointed on 4th October 1977 and arrived to take up his new post on December 1st of that year.

Many other subjects made their first appearance in the years of Mr Macleod's leadership of the school, the following being only some examples: Economics; Economic History; Navigation and Seamanship; Computer Studies; Technological Studies; Geology. The setting up of the Guidance Department and its development was also a feature of the 1970s. The school pioneered many aspects of new ideas in education, also providing many "16 plus" Modules, and inter-departmental courses like Social and Vocational Education. The roll of the school (287 in the Secondary in August 1972) had passed the 500 mark in August, 1980, and along with this increase in pupil numbers went a marked increase in the number of teaching staff. It must be said too that certain subjects disappeared, either because of lack of demand for them or because a teacher solely in charge of a particular subject left the school.

Such growth in pupil and staff numbers, taken together with the appearance of new departments and subjects, naturally placed massive demands on accommodation. There is certainly no doubt that Mr Macleod pushed matters to the limit and beyond in order either to acquire new accommodation or to alter existing parts of the school to meet new demands.

Few, if any, would argue today that the use of computers in schools is a luxury that schools cannot really afford. Mr Macleod's early interest in such matters, and his conviction of their important applications, saw that the school was in the forefront nationally in the introduction of computers in education. It was not long before we saw the results of this work — the school administration became computer based, the pupils enjoyed developing their work with computers, and many teachers took the opportunity to find out the possibilities involved. Many now use word processors in the work of their departments, having a great deal of information on disk. The staff study-base (Another feature appearing during the years 1972 - 86) has a word processor, disk drive and print-out equipment available for all teachers who wish to use it.

There were many other developments of lasting importance which made their first impact during those fourteen years. That the school acquired its own playing fields has been reported in the article on Physical Education. The school's first minibus provided great possibilities. The expansion of the reprographics service has also been noted elsewhere. In matters of school discipline, Fortrose Academy staff discussed the matter of corporal punishment, and voted clearly for the abolition of the belt. It had, in any case, come to be used very infrequently, but the decision to end its use here was an important one. The school year was also changed, the "move-up" for pupils to a new class now taking place around the end of May. This change meant that Primary 7 pupils (whose date for transfer to Fortrose Academy was still at the end of the summer holidays) could now visit the Academy for a whole week, and have a taste of the timetable they would have when they came to Fortrose in August. The "Primary Week" has proved a great success, for the young pupils see for themselves what Secondary Education is like and realise, hopefully, that there is no reason to worry, during the summer, about coming to the Academy! The change has been most beneficial in other ways for it allows pupils in the "new" S5 and S6 an earlier start to their courses and it gives a much greater sense of purpose to the last few weeks before the Summer holidays. The timetable itself was under continuous scrutiny, and it was Mr Macleod who introduced the present system of flexible units of period times, — anything from about 30 minutes upwards.

While on the matter of senior pupils and their timetables, it should be noted that leave of absence was first granted to pupils during these years; pupils taking their S.C.E. examinations were therefore able to study at home if they so wished. They were, of course, welcome to come to school as usual if they so chose. Debate about this leave of absence continues, views being sincerely held for and against the practice. There is no doubt that it does give pupils a greater degree of responsibility for the organisation of their own work, and in this way, they are brought face to face with a form of self-discipline in their own homes — a form of self-discipline which will often be much more difficult to tackle in some far off city with all its attendant attractions to young students.

The foregoing paragraphs have concentrated on a number (though by no means all) of the changes introduced in the years from 1972 to 1986. The introduction of any particular change in itself is not necessarily praiseworthy — for a change might appear far later than should have been the case, and innovations may later be viewed as steps taken completely in the wrong direction. Neither of these charges can be directed against Fortrose Academy during these years. The fact is that the ideas developed were not only highly successful, but also meant that Fortrose Academy actually led the way in pioneering new methods. The years were challenging ones, and schools and rectors across the country had to cope with many other factors besides those mentioned here. The staff and pupils of Fortrose Academy can fairly claim that they were stirred rather than shaken by those formative years.

Many pupils have enjoyed minibus trips over the years. In this picture, taken in May, 1983, IR pupils are enjoying a visit to Stirling to see some of its historical sites. The school actually ran two minibuses for some years.

"DUKE"

C. MACKENZIE

Mr Macleod's dog "Duke" was regarded as a real "character" by many pupils in the school. They thought it was a "good idea having a dog wandering about the school", for it "livened the place up."

Duke appeared to be everything a member of our school community ought to be. He would calmly endure delay in the pursuit of his duties, for, if a door was shut, "he would always wait for someone to come along and open it". His concern for the school was evident, for he "always accompanied Mr Macleod around the school" to see that all was well.

Duke was known to have an interest in sport; "occasionally he joined in the football..." but it appears his attempts to take part were not fully appreciated. Enthusiasm for exercise however, remained for "When Duke saw Mr Macleod coming for his walk, he would go mad and ice-skate on the freshly polished floors." Many pupils, seeking Duke avidly seeking out food, would part with a crisp or two. Duke got on well with everyone — or almost everyone. There was one notable exception, and when this rival dog appeared, Duke's character changed — completely for the worse — as anyone who saw the change from mild dog to wild dog will confirm! The explanation appears to be that the two dogs were rivals for the attentions of a "girl-friend" in the outskirts of Fortrose. The normally well-behaved Duke might, when the bell rang at 4pm, take off towards the Wards area — very inconvenient if his owner had to attend a meeting some distance away after school!

(The quotations about Duke are taken from comments made by pupils of 3R.)

MISS E. MACLEOD

Miss MacLeod began her primary schooldays in Golspie, but a few years later her family moved to the Black Isle and Miss MacLeod, now about half-way through Primary School, found herself a pupil in the nearby school in Munlochy. Miss MacLeod is of course a former pupil of Fortrose Academy and many of her memories are included on other pages; it was of particular interest to hear of teachers still at Fortrose, and of whom I had heard from people who had been pupils in the 1920s. Miss Hepburn was still on the staff when Miss MacLeod arrived to begin her first year at Fortrose, and Miss Noble took her for Latin in the first and second years. The Rector himself, Mr K. Macleod, then took over, teaching Classics through to the sixth year. Miss Bowie was still deeply involved in teaching English and History to the pupils of the senior school.

AVOCH JUNIOR SECONDARY SCHOOL
THE CLOSURE OF ITS SECONDARY DEPARTMENT, 1973.

1973 was a year of great importance to the schools at Avoch and Fortrose. Miss MacLeod had been on the staff of Avoch Junior Secondary School for a number of years, and in August 1973 now arrived to start teaching at the school where she herself had been a pupil. This was brought about by the fact that the Secondary Department at Avoch was closed in 1973, their secondary pupils now coming to Fortrose Academy.

The Fortrose Academy Rector's Log Book has an entry dated 22 August, 1973, which reads:

> "The school re-opened for the new session today. For the first time there is no Primary Department which has amalgamated with Avoch Primary School, pupils from the Fortrose/Rosemarkie area being transported by contract buses.

> Fortrose Academy is now fully comprehensive, receiving all secondary pupils from North Kessock to Cromarty."

The number of (secondary) pupils at Fortrose Academy rose from 287 in Session 1972/73 to 404 in 1973/74. It can reasonably be assumed that there had been some concern in both schools at the loss of these pupils who had now moved away. Miss MacLeod had viewed the change with mixed feelings, for she had thoroughly enjoyed teaching at Avoch from the moment of her arrival. The Secondary Department at Avoch had been of a size small enough for staff to know every pupil really well; a teacher had the same pupils all the way through the secondary. In addition to the subjects taken by the full-time staff, other subjects were taught by itinerant teachers — notably Art, P.E., Home Economics, Technical Education and Music.

In a school in which standards of behaviour were good and pupils happy, there was naturally sorrow that the Secondary Department at Avoch was to close. Miss MacLeod faced the question that always presents itself to teachers returning to work in a school where they had been pupils — would the school she remembered as a pupil be one she could now, as a member of staff, accept and happily teach in? The answer was to be yes. Equally happily, the pupils who came from Avoch's Secondary Department, having recognised the fact of change, settled into Fortrose Academy remarkably well and all put effort into making their days in their new school ones of cheerful co-operation.

Avoch Primary School. (1987).

MR M. MACIVER: RECTOR

Everyone would surely now agree that the study of History involves a great deal more than the mere rote learning of "significant" dates; many would go further and say that there is no need to learn dates at all! This is not to say that students would be unaware of the times at which events happened, for, if interest is stimulated, a sense of time becomes almost instinctive. We can all quote dates instantly — provided they mean something to us.

Thus it happened, on 11th March, 1986, that members of staff in Fortrose Academy each received a letter from Mr D.W. MacLeod, thanking them for their support over the years and informing them that he was to retire at the end of the session. That the departure of one Rector, and the arrival of another, is a most important moment in the history of a school is a view with which few would disagree, and staff, parents and pupils naturally found a great deal of their conversation centred on this most significant piece of news. Many questions were raised, enthusiastically discussed and conclusions drawn. There is no need to describe all the imagined possibilities, for we have now been in a position for some time to deal with the real and the known — the man appointed to be our new Rector — Mr Matthew MacIver.

For some years a most valuable liaison existed between Fortrose Academy and the Nicolson Institute in Stornoway, when pupils from the two schools would meet to take part in a number of matches, notably football and hockey. Pupils from Stornoway would come to Fortrose for a few days, stay in the homes of the Black Isle pupils, enjoy their hospitality and take part in competitive sport. The following year, it would be the Fortrose pupils and staff who would go to Lewis and enjoy their friendly welcome. Unfortunately, these exchange visits have stopped — a great pity, for they gave an opportunity for pupils to take part in matches with teams they would otherwise not see, and enjoy the scenery and friendship which each contrasting area had to offer.

It was on one of these visits to the Black Isle, some twenty three years ago, that the captain of the Nicolson's senior football team was a certain Matthew MacIver! He had for some time taken this game very seriously, and certainly his leadership of the Lewis' team must have been most effective in the match with our pupils, for they beat the Fortrose Academy team 3-1. The young Matthew MacIver had in fact already heard a great deal about Fortrose, for his father was a cousin of Mr W.D. MacPhail, Rector of Fortrose Academy at that time. Such then was our present Rector's first visit to Fortrose Academy!

Mr MacIver had been brought up in the Point district of Lewis and had spent his Primary days at Aird Junior Secondary School before going on to spend six years at the Nicolson Institute. He enjoyed a great deal that his secondary education there had to offer, being most interested in Latin and Maths. He took his "Highers" in the fifth year, and in his sixth year developed the habit of reading to a much greater and wider extent than previously. This in turn led to a strengthened interest in History — so much so that the probable study of Mathematics at University gave way to an Honours Degree course in History, with specialisation in 18th century studies. In his final year, Mr MacIver studied Scottish History, clearly with considerable application and interest, for he won the Scottish History medal. It should also be added that his interest in football during those years remained an active one and he continued to take the game very seriously.

Many people find it difficult to pinpoint the particular moment in their lives when the decision is taken to follow a chosen career. Perhaps no such moment exists for many, the process having evolved over a period of years, so that, as in Mr MacIver's case, the choice of a teaching career seemed a natural progression. He undertook his teacher training at Moray House, being qualified in History and Modern Studies — his qualification in Modern Studies being one of the first formal such certificates; up to that time, it had been assumed that a certificated History teacher would be automatically covered to teach Modern Studies.

Mr MacIver's teaching career began in 1969 — as an assistant teacher of History at Kilmarnock Academy. This was a part of the country to which he had long been attracted and he enjoyed his spell there, relatively short though it was, for he moved to Craigmount High School, Edinburgh, in 1971. This was a brand new comprehensive school, and it was to have a new Principal Teacher of History in 1972, for Mr MacIver was appointed to that post in that year. The school was a large one, its roll peaking at 1,900 pupils. It gave Mr MacIver a very challenging introduction to the duties of a Principal Teacher, for the History Department had eight teachers. The largest second year roll for which he had to plan numbered 494 pupils — almost as large a number as the total roll in Fortrose Academy today. His time-consuming duties did not prevent him from successfully completing a Master of Education degree course during the years 1976 - 79.

1980 saw Mr MacIver make a break with class teaching, for he was appointed Assistant Rector (Curriculum) at the Royal High School, Edinburgh -- incidentally the oldest school of its kind in Scotland. Further promotion was to come quickly, for in 1983, he became Depute Head at Balerno High School. This was a brand new school, and Mr MacIver was appointed eight months before it opened. He was responsible for the entire curriculum structure of the school and all the work this involved, including the preparation of the timetable, an important and vital set of tasks which had to be efficiently completed if the early days of the school's life were to be successful. That the problems were mastered most effectively there is no question, his work there no doubt coming under careful scrutiny when he applied for the post of Rector at Fortrose Academy.

As we know, his application was successful, and he was duly appointed on 19th June, 1986. This was the date on which Fortrose Academy that year held its Sports Day, and a number of parents, pupils and staff caught their first sight of our new Rector on the playing fields! Although Mr MacIver visited the school and met the teachers during one of the in-service days before the pupils returned to school on the 19th August, 1986, he did not actually take over until 15th September, 1986.

One's first impressions — of a person or a place — are always interesting and seem to have a heightened importance at a time when actual extent of practical acquaintance is limited. Certainly there was discussion in plenty about the new Rector, as might reasonably be expected — but what of his first impressions of Fortrose Academy?

Mr MacIver had come to Fortrose from Balerno High School, which, as a brand new school, had been specially designed with the idea of a "Community School" very much in mind. It was open seven days a week, all the year round, and a large number of adults used its facilities. A nursery for children was included, and breakfasts, lunches, teas etc. were served to all comers; adults from the surrounding areas would be welcomed into the staff-room for cups of tea or coffee! Principal Teachers were never allowed to think of the rooms they used as "their" rooms — everything in the school belonged to everybody, and a genuine community spirit was positively sought in an atmosphere of natural openness. Coming from such a school, Mr MacIver must have been immediately aware of the many differences in Fortrose Academy, and he himself says that his first impression was that he was back at the Royal High School in Edinburgh. This was, of course, a very good school. In this sense, Mr MacIver must have felt that in Fortrose Academy, he was in surroundings both familiar and secure!

Although it is clear that schools in the 1980s still differ enormously one from the other, it is equally true that they have also experienced great changes in a variety of ways. Certainly, looking back to his days as a senior pupil in the early to mid 1960s, Mr MacIver can pinpoint some significant developments of those intervening years. Attitudes of teachers towards pupils have changed enormously; pupils are treated, to a much greater extent than ever before, as individuals. Strangely enough, as our new Rector pointed out, it was the formation of the huge comprehensive schools which played a part in this process, for the guidance systems that they produced both initiated and encouraged great changes in the attitudes of all within the schools. Certainly, it must be admitted that guidance staff were at first sometimes viewed with a considerable amount of suspicion, not to say derision, by the established power bases within schools. That those involved in guidance work are now regarded as a necessary, indeed vital, part of a school, is sufficient proof of the value of their work.

Most significant developments have also taken place in schools as a result of discussion of the value of the subjects taught and the principles and techniques of teaching them. If pupils are actively involved in their own education, there should be no need for anyone to be afraid of what teachers call reasonable "working noise", as pupils move about to find material, discuss work in groups, or use the various forms of equipment available, by themselves. Pupils are, more than ever, encouraged to "go out" of the classroom, while visitors to a school are increasingly welcomed.

A direct result of the abundant changes in education was the appearance of an excessive demand on teachers' time. Most would agree with Mr MacIver's view that these most dramatic increases in teachers' workloads were fundamental to the problems of the recent period of unrest among teachers in Scotland. Further, Mr MacIver believes that even yet these demands on teachers are not fully appreciated by many — whether in the public at large or in the higher realms of Scottish educational management. Huge responsibilities for teachers are still to come.

Mr MacIver has now been with us for eighteen months and pupils and staff were early aware of a spirit of continuing innovation and change within the school. Those teachers who were in the school during the years of Mr D.W. MacLeod are of course no strangers to such a situation, which in fact produces a constant self-examination which can do the school nothing but good. Before the 1986 - 87 session had ended, a number of ideas had been discussed by the staff. By a clear, (if not massive) majority, staff voted that the close of session prize-giving would end and in its place there would be held a closing ceremony. This closing ceremony, on 1st July, 1987, marked a clear departure from previous "Prize-givings" — for not only was there no award of prizes, there was no platform party either. The Rector's Report for the session was printed and copies handed out for those present to read, the Rector himself giving a short address on other matters not mentioned in his written report. An interesting feature of the Closing Ceremony was the Former Pupil's Address, this first one being most ably delivered by Miss Petra MacLeod, who had recently left the school. Certainly one feature of previous ceremonies remained — the contributions, most enjoyable as always, from the staff and pupils of the Music Department.

One other idea, which had in fact been discussed on a few occasions dating back a number of years, has now become a fact of school life. This is the setting up of pupil councils, which are elected solely by the pupils, each register class electing two representatives. Three Pupil Councils exist, one for S1,2, one for S3,4 and a Senior Pupil Council. Regular meetings are held, and Minutes are duplicated in order that register classes can air their views on the matters under discussion and thereby let their representatives know the majority view on particular issues. Many items are on the agenda for these meetings — the 5th and 6th year pupil council having discussed topics such as school uniform, the tuck shop, the possibility of re-introducing a prefect system, the authority of senior pupils, the structure of the timetable and transport problems.

A number of other important matters have been, or are being, closely examined by staff. The Guidance system has been arranged on a new basis, and Careers Education, Assessment and the school timetable have been reviewed. In fact, it is clear that Mr MacIver has a particular view of the role of the Rector in a school and sees a rector very much as a "managing", as opposed to "teaching" figure. It is certainly obvious to all, in view of all the new functions carried out by schools, that the days of the "Head" doing everything have gone. Mr MacIver stresses that the industrial action of 1984 - 87 clearly illustrates the need for what he terms "participative management". This means that teachers and pupils must be involved in considering decisions which will affect them; an old style, all powerful Rector — if ever there was such a thing — is certainly long gone.

Mr MacIver has a clear understanding of the changing nature inherent in the Rector's role in the 1980s, a role that, as he pointed out, is liable to move significantly in the near future if the government proposals on the new School Boards take effect. Faced with two masters — the Education Authority on one hand, and the School Board on the other — headteachers could well find themselves in a highly complex situation — to say the least!

3R PUPILS.....
HAVE THEIR SAY!

(The pupils were in 2R when these responses were written — at the end of May, 1987. The decision to compile this unit of work had just been taken, and the chance to canvass all 2R pupils was seized!)

FIRST IMPRESSIONS.........

ALAN ROSS : When I was in Primary School I was the only boy in my year, so my mates were mostly in Pr. 6. This meant when I came to Fortrose I had to make new friends. (I soon overcame this problem). My general impression of Fortrose was: it was very big, with many teachers and pupils, but I liked it. I had never looked forward to going to the Academy but now I never look back.

MAIREAD THIN : My first impression of Fortrose was the sheer size. The 6th years seemed like giants! People seemed to pour from everywhere. One thing I remember very clearly was getting squashed in the corridors!

MORVEN BISSET : My first impressions on arriving at Fortrose were that there seemed hundreds of pupils everywhere and the teachers looked SO serious. I remember looking at one teacher, naming no names of course, and thinking I wouldn't like to get on the wrong side of him!! I thought that everybody looked so settled in and relaxed apart from me, but they weren't really.

TARA GRANT : .....I really liked the canteen because it was like a cafe and you could take what you wanted; in my Primary School you had to take what you were given.

LEE STEWART	:	Before I came to this school I thought it would be terrible with people bossing me about and I thought I would lose my way around. But it was very different. Nobody really bossed me and I only lost my way around once.
DIANE MILLER	:	I thought it was very big; the hall was so big and the noise level was high. Another thing that hit me was the way the tuck shop was so uncontrolled. By the time you got out of the tuck shop, your crisps would be like breadcrumbs and your Mars bar would be as flat as a pancake!
AMANDA REID	:	.....I was a little frightened of the senior pupils but I had plenty of friends because of the musical the Snow Queen. It had pupils from Primary 7 who were going into S1, so we all knew each other.
JOHN FERGUSON	:	The amount of times we moved classes was great and the number of teachers did not make school so boring.
TONY FORSYTH	:	.....I kept getting lost because I wasn't here for the introductory week.....
KEVIN REID	:	My first impression was that it was big and I thought the teachers were terrors, but I was wrong. The first day I started here I got lost. I liked the canteen best.
RACHEL JENNINGS	:	When I first came to Fortrose I was slightly nervous but quite excited with the thought of starting a new timetable with subjects I'd never had before. I thought that the school itself was quite small; I expected it to be a lot larger.
STUART ADAMS	:	When I arrived for the Primary week my first impression of the school was its size. I thought it was very large and I was afraid of getting lost. After the first week I knew where most of my classes were and I had made friends. Most pupils in the school were friendly and kept calling us "little first years". The teachers were all friendly. Mind you, after we had started the new term, I started getting exercises.
JOHN BROOKS	:	My first impressions were that it was big and it was strange that you had to move around to classes and I took a bit of time to get used to the different teachers.

C. MACKENZIE

WHAT I LIKED BEST AT FORTROSE ACADEMY......

NORMA JACK : I liked Duke, Mr MacLeod's dog. He was always wandering about mooching for food, but he was really nice.

SEONAID WALLACE : I liked the meals with a choice and I also liked Duke, and the tuck shop.

MORVEN BISSET : I liked the fact that you didn't have to have the same teacher all day, especially if you didn't like him/her — not that anyone wouldn't like the teachers here!!!!

CHRISTINE SMITH : I liked the L.T.A. on a Friday best. I had never had the chance to choose what I wanted to do for a whole afternoon in school.

JULIE CROMPTON : ...Meeting people and making friends. I also like the idea of pupils meetings, because you can put things forward.

JENNI MACDONALD : The thing I most like about Fortrose Academy is being able to go out of the grounds at lunch-break.

RORY GUNN : The thing I liked most about the school was the range of subjects you got and you also made a lot of friends.

AND WHAT I LIKED LEAST!

ANON : All the homework you get every day; also the punishment exercises.

ANDREA ROSE : The thing I liked least was being parted from your friends that had been your friends for years.

RUTH GORDON : I didn't like the way teachers wanted you to answer a question when you hadn't the faintest idea about the answer. Also, when you knock on a classroom door and wait for an answer, and wait, and wait, and wait, and wait, and wait.........

ANON : The thing I like least about the school is the teachers.

RORY GUNN : It was that in Primary 7 you were at the top of the school, but in Fortrose you were one of the "little first years."

ANON : .....Getting put into different classes; it felt as if we were like cattle and were being herded up into different pens.

121

MY MOST EMBARRASSING MOMENT!

KAREN FIDDES : It was when I knocked one of the teacher's favourite plants off the desk and broke it.

GARY RODWELL : It was when I dropped my tray with my dinner on to the floor.

CHRIS LOWE : .....When I accidentally ran my finger through the sewing machine.

RACHEL JENNINGS : The most embarrassing moment I had was when I called a teacher "Dad" by mistake.

ANON : It was when I was walking down the steps in front of five teachers and I tripped and fell and my skirt split all the way up the back!

CHRISTINE SMITH : When I was talking to a teacher about another teacher and let out the teacher's nickname. The teacher turned round and said "WHAT?!!"

ANON : When I hit a fourth year pupil over the head and was seen by a teacher.

PAUL GRAIZER : It happened when I tried to jump the fence by the path at Greengates; I got my trousers caught and ripped them.

JENNI MACDONALD : My most embarrassing moment in the school was going into a class and sitting on a broken chair; it gave way completely and I landed on the floor.

JANICE FRASER : My most awkward moment was when I was cycling up to school in the winter, when the road was covered in a sheet of ice. My bike slipped away from under me and slid away down the road.

ANON : When I walked into a certain class and it was the wrong class, but I didn't know and the teacher started the lesson. A few minutes later I got up and walked out.

IF I COULD MAKE ONE CHANGE.....

SEONAID WALLACE : I would have 10 minutes in between classes so we can have a rest and a breath of fresh air.

KAREEN MITCHELL : There should be tables and chairs outside in the summer so that people can have their lunch outside.

TARA GRANT : I would sack all the teachers over the age of forty!

GAY PATIENCE : I would sack all the teachers over the age of twenty one.

ALAN ROSS : I would replace all the teachers with robots.

JANICE FRASER : If I had the power to make one change in the school, it would be that there would be no more tests or exams.

TRISHA CATTO : It would be to have lunch from 12 noon to 1pm and have a break sometime between 1pm and 3.45pm.

ANON : I would get the school a 25 metre swimming pool.

MR K. LORRAINE

1959 was an important year for both teachers of History in Fortrose Academy, for we were then pupils at important stages in our respective schools. In June, 1959, I left Mackie Academy, Stonehaven after 13 years as a pupil in its Primary and Secondary Departments, while in August 1959, Mr K Lorraine arrived to start his schooldays at Balgreen Primary School in Edinburgh. All his Primary schooldays were to be spent there, and in Primary 7, he sat the "Eleven Plus" — clearly regarded by all there as an important step, for even the dance at the end of Primary 7 was called the "Qualifying Dance."

Pupils might be surprised to hear that Mr Lorraine began his secondary schooling at Easter, for in the Black Isle pupils start that stage of their education after the Summer holidays. He found himself in what was termed one of the "Prep" classes until the summer holidays, after which he went into the first year proper. After his years at Boroughmuir Senior Secondary, Mr Lorraine went to Edinburgh University, where he studied History and Politics. After graduating, he did not go directly to train as a teacher, but took on a post assisting in the work of the Professor of the History of Science, who was involved in writing a book on the first Astronomer Royal. Besides working on relevant documents, Mr Lorraine's activities also included the actual collection of documents involved in the research — which meant trips to many places, as far away as London.

Training as a teacher in 1977 - 78, Mr Lorraine was naturally interested to see a certain post advertised — that of a History/Modern Studies teacher at Fortrose Academy. He applied, but was told the job had been filled. As matters turned out, that very post became vacant again within three months, and an application was sent north in Mr Lorraine's name — by his tutor at his former College of Education. On the last Wednesday of June, 1978, the phone rang in the Lorraine household in Edinburgh — Mr D.W. Macleod was inviting this newly qualified teacher to attend an interview at Fortrose.

The day on which any person attends an interview is an important one, and it is a time above all when one naturally wants things to go smoothly. Such was not to be the case for Mr Lorraine, for the very beginning of the journey north (or rather what should have been the beginning) proved a genuine non-starter — when the train driver failed to turn up. Faced with this dire situation, many applicants might justifiably have felt a mild sensation of panic, for Fortrose was a fair distance away, involving a number of transport changes — train/bus/ferry/bus — not to mention the chance of missing a connection.

Mr Lorraine was fortunately easily able to deal with the situation and simply secured a seat on one of the flights available from Edinburgh Airport to the Inverness Airport at Dalcross. In fact, this use of speedier transport resulted in Mr Lorraine arriving in Fortrose far too early. This free time was spent pleasantly enough — relaxing at the harbour! After a fairly lengthy interview, Mr Lorraine was offered the post — and accepted. He was to start his teaching in Fortrose Academy in Room 2, but within two years had to face the prospect of teaching in the "demountable" buildings, which had just made their re-appearance.

Teachers are apt to experiment with the layout of their rooms, and Mr Lorraine has good cause to remember one such re-arrangement in Room 32. The very day after he had carried out such a repositioning of desks and chairs, he was checking some pupil's work and went to sit down at his desk — at its former position — and fell flat on the floor! Such was the reverence of the pupils for their teacher (or was it the expression on Mr Lorraine's face?) that not one giggle was heard, the pupils working on in studied silence.

Mr Lorraine has been Assistant Principal Teacher of Guidance since January, 1984; he also has complete responsibility for the organisation of the Modern Studies Department, and in addition teaches in the History Department! He early took an active interest in many aspects of the school's wider activities, one of which is the organisation of school trips abroad, and it was on this subject that I invited him to write the article which follows.

FUN AND GAMES,
SUNSHINE AND SAND,
SNOW AND WIND

	EASTER	SUMMER
1987	Courchevel (France)	
1986	Auris (France)	
1985		Majorca
1984	Valmorel (France)	
1983	Valmorel	Lido de Jessolo (Italy)
1982	Madessimo (Italy)	Spain
1981	Madessimo	Lido de Jessolo
1980		Valkenburg (Holland)
1979		Rome: Sorrento
1978		Paris

Fun and games, sunshine and sand, snow and wind. School trips are all of these — and a lot more. Since arriving at Fortrose Academy, there have been school trips to a variety of places, both at Easter and during the summer holidays. "How can you be bothered?" "How can you put up with 'them'?" parents often ask — 'them' being their own children of course. Well, 'them' are never as bad as parents and staff seem to think they are going to be — or indeed could be. When you consider that on average, only about three or four staff go away with pupils and there have been up to forty of 'them' on a holiday, they behave themselves remarkably well. That's not to say, of course, that nothing goes on 'behind the scenes' — it does. Despite any amount of vigilance and keeping one's ear to the ground, pupils do try it on. Sometimes they succeed, sometimes they don't, but generally, events come to light — it may be several weeks or months afterwards, but they do come to light and 'them' to no harm.

Miss McCulloch and pupils enjoying the Spanish sunshine.

Summer holidays have always been more popular than ski trips at Easter — though the largest group yet was that which went to Auris in 1986 — thirty-nine pupils and three staff. The ski-ing is, quite naturally, very active. The first ever ski trip to Madessimo in 1981 in the Italian Alps was memorable for its lack of snow. The beginners, myself and Miss Aileen Fraser amongst them, may vividly recall the somewhat narrow strip of snow we learnt to snow plough down and were encouraged to come to a halt by the huge pool of melted snow we either missed or got soaked in! For some of us, it was a bit of both. Once we had got the basics learned, we moved up the mountain to what seemed a white paradise — snow and lots of it. But, since that was our first trip, we were not to realise that what we thought of as a lot of snow was in fact, not — subsequent trips taught us that, but ignorance was bliss — in 1981. Yet we must all have enjoyed it as we organised another trip to Madessimo for the following year. Since Madessimo, we have been fortunate in that the resorts we have chosen have all got appreciably better. 1988 will see the return of Fortrose Academy to the slopes of Courchevel, which undoubtedly is the best resort we have visited. The slopes are long, wide and plentiful, short waits at the many lifts and such a variety of runs for skiers of all abilities.

The days are taken up with full-time ski-ing and most of the companies we have dealt with arrange activities for all in the evenings, which are not, of course, compulsory, but are taken up by some in the group. Apart from breakfast, lunch, dinner and last thing at night, it is an opportunity to do something together as pupils ski in their groups in the mornings and

Anna Dove; Terry Owens; Georgia Tilbrook; Mr D. Mackenzie; Jill McFarlane; Kate Dove; Joanna Croson.

afternoons, receiving lessons at some time during the day. The first few days of any trip always, but always, hear plenty moans and groans about the rooms, the food, nothing to do at night, 11pm curfews and whatever else comes to mind. However, by the end of it all, regrets about going home (usually, but not always!!) and hopes that parents might see their way to financing a trip the following year, are expressed.

Summer trips, on the other hand, are much more restful. Everyone goes basically for the sunshine and sand, although the school's last summer trip was more active — windsurfing and tennis lessons were arranged for those who wanted to exert themselves. Day or half-day outings can be arranged for those that wish to venture forth and no doubts about it, the outings to Venice when in Lido de Jessolo were for me anyway, those which stand out in my mind. Venice was not the dirty, smelly city of canals at all — it's one of the most marvellous places I've been fortunate enough to visit. Yes, if you do sit down to have a snack in St Mark's Square or take a gondola, you are ripped off, but there are plenty places off the main thoroughfare where you can eat at reasonable prices. A city full of history, but no lessons given; just time — not enough of it — to see around the place. A visit to the world famous glass factory, where the heat was unbearable, to St Mark's Basilica, where the cool was more than welcome, the Doge's Palace, Rialto Bridge, Bridge of Sighs and much, much more.

The sun and heat are always a pleasure to go for, though some return with a bit more of the former than they bargained for, or were warned about. During the last summer trip organised by the school to Majorca in 1985, removing sea urchin spines from feet (on one occasion, even having to get to the 'bottom' of those black spikes) became an almost daily task. Yet on all our organised trips abroad, there have never been — touch wood!! — any accidents of a serious nature — with one exception. On the ski trip to Auris, someone came to a sudden halt on the last day and found himself in some pain with badly torn ligaments in the left knee, resulting in the left leg being in plaster for three weeks on return to school.

Everyone enjoys a good holiday and on the whole school trips have been enjoyed by those who go on them, staff and pupils alike. Yes, there are times when you wonder if it was worth it all whilst you are there, 'them' are inconsiderate and you wish they were at home, too, but all in all I would be telling a lie if I said that school trips are not memorable, for various reasons, for all included. If the reader has been on such a trip, I hope they would agree.

126

PLAIN SAILING?
SIXTH YEAR PUPILS, DIANNE PATIENCE AND DEBBIE STAINES REVIEW THEIR "FORTROSE YEARS".

This session, we (Dianne Patience and Debbie Staines) had the opportunity of introducing the Primary 7 pupils of Avoch School to Fortrose Academy. For the majority of them, secondary school seemed more than a little daunting. But in 1982, what were our first reactions.....?

"To be honest, I (Dianne) was petrified!! In contrast to the relaxed atmosphere of Avoch Primary, Fortrose seemed to be run by an iron fist. The actual size of both school and pupils was pushed to the back of my mind as we were given a taste of the lessons to come — resulting in my returning home to astonish everyone with my French repertoire of 'bonjour' and 'ça va'.

I (Debbie) didn't arrive at Fortrose until 1984. I couldn't believe it when I entered the school to see a dog sprawled outside the office. At first I thought my nerves were playing up, but as Mr Macleod came out to greet us with a doggie biscuit in his hand, I decided this 'mad house' was for me.... My last school, Golspie High, was smaller than Fortrose and I felt sure that an ordnance survey map would be needed, for the first month at least.

What we have enjoyed most about school.......

Well, the 'less academic' side of our education has been varied and enjoyable. Creative aesthetic courses gave pupils in years 3 and 4 the opportunity to participate in subjects that may not otherwise be included in their academic curriculum — eg. computing, art, drama, creative dance and music. It gave us a chance to express ourselves in more interesting ways, although it was sometimes extremely embarrassing pretending to be a cow or a bird in front of the drama class!!

Leisure has also been good fun and another chance to try new sports and hobbies or to improve upon familiar ones. A recent addition to the leisure range is Community Service which involves helping various groups in the Black Isle community. Over the past two months in this leisure we have been attending Avoch Primary to assist with various age groups within the school. We also believe that this experience may help us in our search for permanent employment when we leave Fortrose.

When I was but a naïve 3rd year pupil, I decided to take advantage of this Leisure system and learn something new. My sailing experiences were on the whole very interesting although I don't think I ever went home dry, nor will I ever sail around the world single-handed!!

On the other hand, certain aspects of school life have been less enjoyable, like cross country during the winter, when it nearly always snowed as soon as we left the changing rooms. Dinner time was also a frustrating time of day in junior school. It seemed to us that our year was always the last to be called in.

Various activities out of school hours have been organised. We have played in hockey and basketball teams, and were in fact part of the team which travelled to play in Aberdeen last year. In an effort to get fit (fitter we should say) we went jogging early (very early) each morning if the weather was fine. Fortunately it frequently rained and so we had a cup of tea instead. Another activity which has always been found enjoyable has been the musicals.

Sports Day has always been an event to look forward to as well as dread. Being roped in to run the 800 metres when you find it hard getting up the stairs can prove to be something of an ordeal! On the other hand, sitting watching all those masculine legs(!) while eating numerous bags of sweets is quite a consolation!

School dances are a good chance to watch the teachers 'enjoying' themselves after their stressful day. Their Can-Can is always amusing to say the least and their dancing is even more of a scream, although it must be said, the aperitifs beforehand do make jiving just a little easier.

Different crazes have come and gone throughout our days at Fortrose, including water balloons, birthday 'clarting', the dreaded chicken scratching, and the most recent, which surprisingly has broken out in the staffroom, not the playground. What more could it be than that extremely stimulating game — Bridge...

Additions to school activities have made it more enjoyable in many ways. The modules provide a wider scope of learning, for example we are doing the Financial Record Keeping module, followed by Law, something we have never had the chance to do before. Also, there are pupil councils which give us the opportunity to voice our opinions, and are encouraging us to try and improve the school.

Over the years, it must be admitted that our attitudes to school have changed — indeed for the better. Student/teacher relations tend to improve as you progress through the school as teachers' attitudes towards you get better and in return you get on well with your teachers. This does help to make school far more enjoyable.

Life at school hasn't always been plain sailing, though, or plain walking as the case may be.... when one Friday, a vain attempt, after our ramble, was made to reach the school — for the buses — by cutting through a field. Had we known what would happen we would have brought suitable camouflage!! Anyway, an essay wasn't THAT bad when you consider what could have happened, as the date was Friday 13th.......

When Mr Macleod left, we were very sad because we had a lot of respect for him. He was always very kind and helpful. But we would also like to say that Mr MacIver has filled his place very well and has brought a new dimension to school life in Fortrose.

We would like to close by saying that when we leave we will fondly look back on our days of 'learning' at Fortrose Academy. (We never thought we'd ever say that when we came here first). We've made the most of our days at Fortrose. After all, these are the best days of our lives!

MRS K. MUNRO: SCHOOL SECRETARY

Mrs Munro is a former pupil of Fortrose Academy, having arrived in the Primary Department as a nine year old, then progressing through the Secondary Department, from which she left at eighteen. Mrs Munro recalls that, at that time, most pupils left school when they reached 14 years of age as there was no shortage of jobs, and they had perhaps to augment the family income. Some very able pupils also left without completing their secondary education simply because their parents didn't have the resources to send them to University or College.

Schools generally reflect the values of the society in which they exist and Mrs Munro agrees that, as a pupil, life in general seemed very highly regulated, school life being no different. Discipline was very strict both within and outwith the classroom. Secondary pupils had to line up in their year groups before going to classes, and Mrs Munro recalls a story that one janitor — apparently an ex-army major — used to parade up and down the lines with a cane; if any pupil's stance was not sufficiently erect, there would be trouble! Similarly, in the classroom, nobody would dare to slouch when replying to a teacher's question.

Mrs Munro confirms that in her schooldays, pupils from outlying areas cycled to school everyday, from as far afield as Cromarty, and in all kinds of weather. If arriving soaked to the skin, they would be sent to the underground boiler-house to dry off. The terrible smell of anthracite gas in the boiler-house was difficult to forget!

Mrs Munro's first post as School Secretary began in 1953 on a part-time basis. She worked 10 hours per week, from 9.30 to 11.30 on each weekday morning, sharing the school office with the Rector, Mr MacPhail, and, in fact, shared the same desk. The main duties then were the collection of lunch money from both primary and secondary departments, the collation of requisition orders and the typing of the Rector's letters and examination papers for all departments. Although leaving the post in 1959, Mrs Munro had clearly enjoyed her work, for she accepted a similar position at Avoch Junior Secondary School, where she worked 6 hours per week — from 9.30 to 12.30 on Mondays and Thursdays, again sharing the Headmaster's office. Mrs Munro remained there until 1973, when she was appointed Secretary at Fortrose Academy, the post being a full-time one. Actual daily hours have varied since the early 1970s, but in 1988 they are from 8.30am to 4.30pm.

It is a fact that all those concerned with secretarial work have found themselves adjusting considerably to meet the demands of new technology used in the administration of business, and in many senses a school is a business, the efficient management of which is vital. One instance of this in Fortrose Academy may be seen in the many sources from which sums of money arrive at the school office. (A Regional directive makes it clear that all such monies are to be handed in to the Secretary, to be lodged in the School Fund Account). Some such sources from which money is dealt with may be listed: School Musicals; School trips; the sale of "Contact"; sale of photographs; school money-raising events; the sale of Christmas cards; use of the school minibus; the hire of disco equipment; staff presentations; private photocopying; private telephone calls; leisure time activity levy. It is plain that a substantial amount is handled each year.

Over the years, more and more paper work has been, and is being, done. Some of these duties include:

School requisition — (Organisation, collation, correspondence, certification of invoices, keeping capitation balance sheets etc.)
Payment of accounts from the school fund.
Sorting, screening and distribution of incoming mail.
Staff members' (teaching and non-teaching) absence and return to duty forms.
Supply teachers' claim forms.
School cleaners' appointment and resignation forms.
Fuel return forms.
School lets forms.
Leisure Instructors' pay claims.
Dealing with enquiries from staff, parents and pupils.
Some statistical returns.
Free school meals forms.
Letters to parents about Medical Inspection and B.C.G.'s
Typing of Rector's confidential reports, letters etc.
And many other secretarial duties!

I am not aware that any count has ever been taken of the number of callers to the school office in the course of a day. Teachers call in for a number of reasons — perhaps simply to collect the minibus keys, or to hear the reply to varied enquiries they have made. Without doubt there are many requests for information, and they often need immediate attention — as does the ringing of the telephone — so that other ongoing work might appear to be held up. Fortunately, the ability to tackle two or three jobs at once is something our school secretaries over the years seem to have mastered. The School Office is now well-equipped with modern technology, and if the work hasn't become easier, it has without doubt become more exciting!

PUPILS OF '88
A SURVEY OF 2R

A great deal of effort is expended today in studying, speaking and writing about young people. The "teenager" has become the object of close scrutiny for a number of reasons; certainly the particular problems of those years seem, quite rightly, to be discussed more openly than ever before. That youthful group too, is an obvious target at which much advertising is directed, and the level of teenage spending in this country has certainly never been higher. The role of youth in History too is an important one. It seems quite appropriate, therefore, that some space be devoted to consider certain aspects of the lives of our pupils in 1988.

Pupils in the second year — they are shown in the photographs — were invited to answer a number of questions. Owing to absence, not all pupils were involved, but replies were returned from 101 pupils. It was emphasised that no names would be published and that pupils need not answer a particular question if they did not want to do so. The temptation to carry out a very detailed survey was resisted, and the number of questions put to our pupils was strictly limited — about a dozen questions being asked, of which nine are here considered. Replies gave very interesting information, some of which can be most useful in our History classes when investigating the lives of young people in earlier decades of this century.

TRAVEL – ABROAD

Communications in various forms, past and present, have frequently featured in the work of our History classes. Modern times have seen a spectacular "boom" in travel, with an ever increasing number of people enjoying the ability to journey with ease to places near and far. The experiences of our second year pupils certainly reflect this trend, almost half the pupils having been abroad.

Understandably, the European countries are the main attraction for our pupils, with 26 having been to France, some on a number of occasions. Spain is also popular, with 14 pupils having enjoyed its attractions. Italy, Belgium, Germany and Switzerland come next, all enjoying virtually the same number of visits from our pupils, followed by Portugal, Yugoslavia, Austria and Cyprus.

No fewer than 20 other countries have had a "single pupil visit" — countries from Canada to Corsica, the Falklands to Fiji, Singapore to Sweden, Norway to New Zealand.

Air travel holds no fear for our 2R pupils — although it must be pointed out that not all pupils going abroad travel by air, for of the pupils who have visited foreign countries, 10 have never flown. Those who have not yet ventured to foreign lands will hopefully have plenty of opportunities to do so in the future, if they so wish.

TRAVEL - TO SCHOOL

A very important, if less spectacular aspect of travel is the question of conveyance to school itself. Provision of transport has improved enormously over the years, and there is no question today of pupils having to walk long distances to school, or to wait for hours after four before boarding a bus for home! This is just as well, for of the 101 pupils surveyed, no fewer than 61 arrive in a bus (full size), their boarding point being within walking distance from their homes. A further 10 pupils also use one of the larger buses during part of their journey to and from school, the other form of transport being a car (3 pupils), minibus (5 pupils) or bicycle (2 pupils). 21 pupils walk to school, 6 cycle all the way, and 2 arrive by car. For those readers adding up the figures, there is one pupil's transport unaccounted for — and it's a minibus for the whole journey!

POCKET MONEY

This is a very difficult area in which anything specific can be safely said, for the circumstances in which, and for which, money is given vary greatly. It is however clear that almost everybody in 2R undertakes a number of jobs around the house or garden etc. in return for the money received. About 15 pupils get no pocket money on a regular basis, but their parents buy them small items when they want, or when they need, something. Certainly the largest category (54 pupils) receive (or "earn") £1 - £2 per week. A number of pupils get much more than this, and for those (about 15) who get £5 a week, prospects at first seem rosy; it should quickly be made clear that this amount has to cover the cost of specific purchases — eg. buying school lunches, clothes or shoes, etc. Once such necessary deductions are made, amounts remaining hovered around the £1.50 mark per week.

WHERE THE MONEY GOES....

Clothes and other items worn by pupils (eg. badges, jewellery, make-up) account for a great deal of pupils' money, no fewer than 40 mentioning this as their main form of purchase. Closely following, come sweets, crisps, fizzy drinks etc., 35 pupils listing these as a favourite purchase. A third major category includes games of various kinds (electronic, computer) models (aircraft, lead figures) and sports, followed by records and cassettes. Spending on reading material (books, comics, magazines) and pets are two more easily distinguishable groups. Then follow huge varieties of all kinds of things on which pocket money is spent — far too varied to list, although some sound intriguing — what is the "something really big" for which one of our hopefuls is saving?

LEISURE HOURS

Black Isle pupils should be very fit if the lists of 2R's favourite pastimes are anything to go by, for no fewer than 75 of our pupils mentioned some form of sport or similar physical activity. Not surprisingly, the most popular was football (15 pupils), followed by horse-riding (12 pupils), then swimming, badminton and athletics (8 pupils for each). Another 14 pastimes involving a fair degree of exertion were named, including hockey, basketball, golf and tennis.

Looking after pets, interest in computers and watching television were the most popular of the remaining groups. There is no doubt that those in 2R are interested in a large and most varied collection of leisure pursuits, for 30 different activities were listed.

MOST VALUED POSSESSION?

The evidence is clear here — our pupils like animals, for 34 considered their pets to be their most valuable possession. The kinds of animal varied enormously — of the 34 listed, there were 11 dogs, 9 cats, 4 horses and a number of others including goldfish, rabbits, sheep and ferrets. Bicycles formed the next major group, with 11 enthusiasts expressing this view; 8 pupils seem to be hankering for the past, for their most prized possession is none other than their teddy — most of which were named! 8 also named their computer, and the same number opted for pieces of jewellery. The remaining prized articles included around 30 different items ranging from a boat, a motorcycle and a car body-shell to savings in the bank, golf clubs and books.

Finally it should be made clear that we were discussing material possessions; other areas of life are much more important to our pupils (eg. Health, Family, Friends) and this was in fact pointed out by the pupils in class.

FAVOURITE POP STAR OR GROUP

It might be expected that, faced with this question, our 2R pupils would, at last, come up with only a few names, each star having a large following in the second year at Fortrose. It was not to be the case, for, our pupils, clearly people of independent judgement, were not to be swayed by national trends, and mentioned no fewer than 44 different groups or pop stars, of which 28 were named by one person only. Admittedly 15 listed Madonna as their favourite, with 10 preferring "Queen", 6 going for Bon Jovi, and Europe, Def Leppard and Iron Maiden each winning 5 votes.

MOST POPULAR TV PROGRAMME

No one programme could command the devoted support of anything like one half, or even one quarter of the second year pupils. Of the 39 programmes they named, the most frequently mentioned was "Bread", with 12 votes. In fact, comedy programmes secured top ratings from 28 pupils who listed such diverse shows as "The Golden Girls", the "Flintstones", and "Blackadder II".

Of the "soaps", "Eastenders" was by far the most popular, with 11 votes. Police/detective style programmes of varying kinds cropped up, "The Equaliser" and "Bergerac" being two examples, although none were as well liked as "Moonlighting".

FORTROSE ACADEMY: CENTENNIAL CELEBRATIONS!

How would you like to celebrate the school's 100th Anniversary on this site?

We can probably all think of a very popular answer to this question! Yes — A Holiday. No fewer than 33 pupils favoured this as a very good way by which to mark the occasion. 10 pupils suggested a day off; 19 pupils, whose enthusiasm was perhaps beginning to cloud reality, proposed a week's break; a further 4 pupils, by now deep in some hopeless dream, put forward even longer periods off school.

The most popular suggestion by far, came from around 45 pupils; it was that a "huge", "giant", "massive", "enormous" (to use but four of our pupils' adjectives) gathering be held in the school grounds. This great event would be in the form of a "party", a "fete", a "festival" or a "carnival" — or all four put together, plus a disco, whatever that would be called!

A recurring idea was that all former pupils and teachers should be specially invited to take part in our celebrations, and that, whatever form the festivities might take, one (or more) famous people should be invited along to open the main event. Our pupils had several ideas about whom their special guests should be; included were members of the Royal Family, Members of Parliament, Sports personalities and T.V. and Pop stars and groups of varying kinds.

One other frequently mentioned idea is summed up in one pupil's response:
> "Have History repeated — the opening of the school done again as it was in 1892, with everyone dressed as they were at that time."

A similar suggestion was that the school should have an Open Day, with special exhibitions showing the History, work and all other aspects of the life of the school displayed for all visitors to examine. Nor were the school buildings themselves forgotten, a few pupils thinking of celebrating, not as some others suggested with firework displays, bonfires, rodeos (!), and Pop concerts, but with the extension of the accommodation, or the addition of a swimming pool.

Pupils were keen that something be done for the future, and another thought was that Tree-planting around the school's boundaries and playing fields would be worthwhile. Last of all, that ever-present sign of birthday-celebration was of course considered — we should have the biggest 100th birthday cake ever seen in the Black Isle!

ANY QUESTIONS?

Our 2R pupils were given the opportunity each to ask one question about the school. How many of their questions shown below can you answer?

1. Where is the time capsule?
2. How much does it cost to run the school for one week — in 1988?
3. How many pupils were there in the 1890s?
4. What famous people have visited the school?
5. How much is the school worth today in £'s?
6. What teacher has been here the longest?
7. Who was the first pupil to enter the school in 1892?
8. What funny things have happened to the teachers that were not meant to happen?
9. What did the first school badge look like?
10. Are we ever going to get a swimming pool?
11. When's it going to close down?
12. How many teachers did the school start with and how many are there today?
13. Who is the school's most famous former pupil still living?
14. What is the worst catastrophe that has ever happened to the school?
15. Why is it that in the summer holidays it is usually raining and we have to stay in, and maybe wish we were back at school, and when it's sunny we're usually cooped up in classrooms?

THE SCHOOL BUILDINGS: 1970-82

The picture shows the new block being built in the early 1970's. It was first used by the Primary Department, before its move to Avoch. (The former Primary accommodation at the Academy was at that time being converted for use by the Technical Education Department.) Secondary staff and pupils moved into the new block at the start of the session in 1973. It contained rooms at that time for the Maths, Art, Classics and Social Subjects Departments.

The new block photographed in 1987.

The picture above shows the return of the demountable buildings — in the late seventies. The "music caravan" is also to be seen.

The view of the school shows the other two blocks of huts which were ready for use by January, 1982. The brick structure close to the fence was an incinerator. It disappeared in seconds, carried off by the heavy machinery which arrived in August 1987 to prepare the area for the new road and car park shown below.

The articles describing the buildings have dealt only with the major developments. There have been many internal alterations, notably since the early 1970's, which are not described here; neither has there been any attempt to describe the changes in departmental accommodation over the years. A description of all the changes in these two categories would require an additional magazine!

A second gymnasium was also built in the early 1970's. This aerial photograph was taken by "Skyviews and General Ltd." It gives a very good picture of the layout of the school around 1973.

MR H. PATIENCE

There are some people in the school who have been pupils and/or members of staff under the direction of no fewer than three Rectors. Such a record would not be difficult to claim for Mr W.D. MacPhail retired in 1972, and Mr D.W. Macleod in 1986. There are however few who can claim to have worked in the school under four Rectors. Mr Patience, our Janitor, is one of the very few members of the present staff who have achieved this Fortrose Academy feat! There is another "record" which Mr Patience holds — he is the full-time member of our staff who has the longest period of continuous service in the school, for he began work here on the 6th February, 1961. Bearing in mind too that Mr Patience spent some time in Fortrose Academy during the years of the Second World War, there is no doubt that his knowledge of the school and its development would be most valuable in this unit of work, and this has proved to be the case, for a great deal of his information has been used throughout, especially in consideration of the buildings.

Mr Patience was born and brought up in Avoch and attended Avoch Public School. (The school buildings have now disappeared, having been demolished some years ago). In an area whose links with the sea were, and are, so important, it was not surprising to hear that the teaching of Navigation was an important feature in the curriculum of the school; Mr Patience estimates that, when he was a boy at this school, there must have been 20 - 30 men from Avoch who had a mate's or skipper's ticket.

Mr Patience arrived as a pupil in Fortrose Academy in 1942. The Rector's Log Book gives a detailed account of the effects of the Second World War on the school, and it was particularly valuable to hear a former pupil's memories of those years, in particular, of the fact that there were quite a number of aircraft in the area, not to mention a few aircraft crashes. On one occasion, a "Tiger Moth" made a forced landing in the Firth, fairly close to the shore, between Avoch and Fortrose; the young Hugh Patience had seen the aircraft going down and naturally made haste to the area, "forgetting" that he should have been returning to classes! He saw the two airmen, who had escaped unhurt from their aircraft, paddling their dinghy towards the shore and was caught up in the excitement of the scene when he was spotted by a recently-retired teacher in the area, taken back to school, and given the belt! The Rector's Log Book refers to the formation of an Air Training Corps in the Academy and one of Mr Patience's memories of Mr K. Macleod is of the Rector dressed in Air Force blue. During the war years posters encouraged everyone to "Dig for Victory" and the pupils of the Academy acted on this advice and grew a variety of vegetables in the area used as the "school garden". This was on a piece of ground stretching from the front of the houses towards the High Street end of Academy Street, and the shore. There were large numbers of forces' personnel in the area, of course, and a number of houses were taken over by the military authorities. This also explains the fact that, as Mr Patience confirms, the Drill Hall was not then used for "gym". It was actually while still at Avoch Public School, in Primary 7, that Mr Patience got his only sight of enemy action, for an enemy aircraft, perhaps after attacking Invergordon, actually made a low level pass over the Black Isle, and machine-gunned a cottage near Corrachie farm. A boy brought to the school some of the smashed bullets that had hit the stone areas of the house!

Leaving Fortrose Academy, Mr Patience was involved in the fishing industry until 18, when he joined the army for three years of National Service, during which time he was posted to various areas in Italy, Germany, Austria and Holland. He returned to his fishing work in 1949, leaving it to come to Fortrose Academy on 6th February, 1961. There was of course no janitor's house at that time, and Mr Patience travelled from Avoch — for a number of years by bicycle, until his purchase of a Morris Minor brought a much more comfortable form of transport. (Many people associate Mr Patience with a blue Morris; this was actually his second "Minor", and a great car it turned out to be, for it served the Patience family faithfully for 17 years!)

A great deal has been said of the accommodation difficulties faced by pupils and staff in the years before the new buildings of the 1960's made their appearance; Mr Patience commented on some of the problems faced by those involved in staging school musicals in the early sixties. These shows were performed in the Town Hall and seats were completely "sold out"! All participants used their ingenuity to produce a colourful performance at minimum cost. The backcloth for one of these early sixties' musical shows (pictured in this magazine) was actually an old railway goods van cover. It was hung outside one of the huts and painted — most effectively too, as the photograph shows. A bus was parked outside the Town Hall and was used as changing accommodation etc. for the members of the cast, who, in order to remain unobserved by the audience, had to climb in and out of the Town Hall through a kitchen window!

The new building work of the mid-sixties must clearly have involved all staff in a fair degree of additional effort. Any teacher who has had to flit from one room to another area in the school knows only too well the unimagined amount of work it actually entails. Certainly the move into the new buildings, at the end of 1965, must have provided a considerable task. The new building had first to be cleaned thoroughly after the builders and other workmen had left, and the floors polished. Huge amounts of supplies had already arrived — desks and chairs, for instance — and with the help of some of the pupils, had been unloaded, unpacked and taken to the appropriate rooms. Mr Patience had of course to check the safe arrival of all incoming goods — a time-consuming task. Each department had ordered what it needed and this had to be correctly distributed. Fortunately, everything arrived on time — and in good order, with no damage to furniture in transit. We must remember too that after staff and pupils entered the brand new buildings, work began on the reconstruction of the "old" building, and this too meant additional work for Mr Patience and his staff. Everyone however, must have been delighted to see the disappearance of the "chicken-runs" — a term, as Mr Patience recalls, used to describe the huts of that time!

Today the school buildings of the sixties still maintain their attractive appearance: eleven cleaners work an average of two hours each per day to keep the buildings clean and tidy for us all. Vandalism is not a major problem in the school, expected "wear and tear" being responsible for most maintenance or renewal work; swing-type doors, for instance, need attention from time to time. Ageing of equipment is an important factor and items of more recent design might perhaps be more economic. The boilers and pumps have now seen quite a number of years of service! An efficient single system of heating throughout the school might be an improvement; the "huts" alone use storage heaters. Mr Patience is also responsible for the care of the school grounds, and their attractive appearance plays no small part in giving everyone a sense of welcome to the school.

It is not surprising that someone who has completed 27 years in the school holds a high opinion of its role. Mr Patience's own family comprises one son and three daughters, all of whom have been educated here. Occasionally we might see Mr Patience walking round the buildings with some of his grand-children — two boys and three girls! Those members of staff who worked in the school when its Primary Department still existed would agree with Mr Patience that one of the school's most pleasant features lay in seeing the infants growing up and progressing through the senior years of their education — by which time members of staff could almost tell what the pupils were thinking!

The reprographics room is always busy! Mrs M. Moir joined us in 1979 on a full-time basis, and Mrs K. Patience arrived in 1985. An extremely sophisticated photocopier is used to provide approximately forty thousand photocopies per month. In addition to a variety of other duties, registration is completed here and the needs of the sick attended to!

"£ POWER!"

That Fortrose Academy pupils enter with enthusiasm into the business of raising money for others was clearly demonstrated on 12th February, 1988. This was "Comic Relief" day, when many of our pupils arrived in class with red noses of various kinds, keen to take part in collecting money for victims of famine in Ethiopia and the Sudan, and for young people in harsh circumstances in Britain. No one who saw the comic capers of that day could doubt that the pupils were most original and vigorous in their money-raising schemes! The pupils have in fact taken part in many fund-raising activities for a great number of good causes.

At the end of the session, in June 1987, many pupils were to be seen in the playing fields in the "Adopt a Sport" campaign; this involved 20 circuits of the running track, and money raised went to support the 1988 British Olympics teams, and the school. Participants were photographed with the famous ice-skater, Karen Barber. The pictures here show four of the pupils taking part. Left: Helen Thornton and Shona Harper; both of 2R. Right: Christine Smith 3R, and Adele Cameron 2R.

Pupils raise money for various school activities and necessary purchases. On 2nd October, 1987, a major programme of sponsored events was organised and all pupils at school on that day took part in an activity of their choice. The variety of events included a sponsored work out, work in, music practice, typing session, cycle, swim, silence, pancake toss, sail, run, horse ride, and walk! The afternoon provided a real "sense of occasion", the great majority of pupils undertaking the sponsored walk. The afternoon was also financially a great success — over £3,300 being raised!

A great deal of money has to be raised to maintain a minibus for school use. There is no doubt that such a vehicle is of great value, and is used by a large number of the staff greatly to extend the educational opportunities of pupils. The P.T.A. takes a particular and practical interest in the effort to provide the school with this vital asset.

In December, 1987, the proceeds of the school's production "A Masque for Christmas" were donated to the R.S.S.P.C.C. for its use at its Killen Centre.

These examples of fund-raising are only a few illustrations of the many ways in which pupils, parents and staff enjoy taking part in a diversity of events, from individual efforts to "whole school" activities.

The photograph here shows a number of pupils (mostly cyclists) preparing to set off on that Friday afternoon, which was fortunately a day of reasonably good, calm weather.

Here are some 3R pupils, pictured on an outing to visit points of interest in connection with the former Black Isle Railway. The pupils are, from the left: *Kevin Reid, John Shepherd; Moray Mackay; Iain McGhee; Andrew Taylor; Alan Whyte; Steven MacIver; Alastair MacLeod; Wendy Jack; Gary Rodwell; Louisa Patience; Lynn Kershaw; Andrea Dalgetty; Maree McDonald. (Absent: Karen Fiddes.)*

This is part of a photograph taken by Mr Ian Rhind, Culbokie. It shows three of our contributors — Miss A. Fraser, Mr D. W. Macleod, and Craig Mackenzie. It was taken during a ceremony in which a major donation was handed over to the Highland Hospice Appeal. Performances of "Annie" had raised the £1,000 donated to this cause.

MR A.G. MACKENZIE

All those former pupils who were in the school between 1953 and 1982 will undoubtedly have memories of Mr A.G. MacKenzie which are particularly clear. Certainly, as far as all our contributors are concerned, memories abound and anecdotes there are in plenty! It is evident that he was able — over a period of many years which saw different styles of teaching — naturally to capture the interest of his pupils: they recall the distinctive manner of his teaching, with its enthusiasm and its humour. Staff too, and former members of staff can confirm that his ability to remain calm under the most trying of circumstances was a most reassuring feature in our Depute Rector!

It was with this last named characteristic in mind that Mr MacKenzie was asked to write a four thousand word account of his experiences in education! This request was a most audacious one, for its completion must involve a great deal of time-consuming effort. Yet such an article, over such a period, would be of great value in bringing together a number of themes.

Mr MacKenzie most kindly agreed to write such an article, and it now follows.

FIFTY YEARS IN SCHOOL

As the subject of this project is the history of a school and as my association with schools has covered the years 1923 to 1982 with a wartime break of five years 1940 - 45, it would perhaps be worthwhile for purposes of comparison and understanding of developments if, before dealing with experiences of Fortrose Academy, I should record impressions of schools in an entirely different environment — as a pupil in an elementary (later called Primary) school in central Glasgow in the 1920s, then as a pupil in a Higher Grade (later Secondary) school in suburban Glasgow in the 1930s, as a student in Glasgow University in the late 1930s, again in University and Teacher Training College in the late 1940s, as Assistant Teacher of English and History in Inverness Royal Academy 1947 - 1953, as Principal Teacher of English subjects in Fortrose Academy 1953 - 1963, and as Depute Rector and Principal Teacher of English again in Fortrose Academy 1963 until retirement in 1982.

Elementary education covered the years 1923 - 1930. Strongest recollections of infant class are the scrape of slate pencil on slate, the smell of plasticine and the bright colours of crayons which were the only media of expression given to us. It is likely that the content of that early education differed only slightly from schooling in Fortrose, but organisation would differ greatly, mainly because of the difference in numbers. In the elementary school which I attended all classes (each of more than 30 pupils) had a teacher and a classroom. It is likely that in Fortrose some classes would be combined. For teachers the principal aids to teaching were blackboard and chalk, perhaps some wall-posters, maps for geography lessons and a piano for singing lessons. Pupils had books and jotters which they had to provide for themselves. It was not until the mid-1930s that text-books were provided by Glasgow Corporation Education Authority and the provision of free milk for everyone was also introduced then. Prior to that time there was a system whereby free books and, in some areas of the city, free clothing were supplied to those in need — which created in a very stark way a picture of the class division which existed in the 1920s, for the free clothing was quite distinctive (school-board suits they were called). The teaching and learning of English was very much a Reading, Writing, Grammar and Spelling routine with a strong emphasis on drilling in parsing of parts of speech and analysis of sentences — simple, complex, compound — use of spelling lists which were issued as home-work and tested in class the following day. Dictation was a weekly exercise as was written composition. Committing to memory of passages of poetry was a feature of the poetry lesson. It is remarkable how readily one can recall long passages of poetry learned by heart at that early age. Narrative poems were the favourite choice — Lord Ullin's Daughter, Wreck of the Hesperus, Charge of the Light Brigade, Hiawatha etc. but some lyrical poems were also chosen... "I wish I lived in a caravan, With a horse to drive like a pedlar man..." In Arithmetic a similar drilling was the practice — the learning of tables — two times table up to the twelve times table. Weights and measures tables were also learned by heart, and training in Mental Arithmetic was a feature of the counting process. (E.g. a doz. articles at $6^3/_4$d each = 6/9; a ton of coal at 3/6 per cwt. = £3.10/-) These examples, of course, were based on the duodecimal coinage with twelve pence in the shilling and twenty shillings in the pound.

Elementary education ended with a Qualifying examination, set, I think, on a regional basis. This exam consisted of a paper in English, including Composition, grammar, poetry, dictation, and a paper in Arithmetic, including ten questions in Mental Arithmetic. Result of this examination determined (1) one's promotion to and placing in the Higher Grade school or (2) placing in an Advanced Division school, or (3) retention in elementary school for a further year. (The Advanced Division school was a two-year secondary which may have been peculiar to Glasgow and which was a kind of forerunner of the Junior Secondary idea.)

The transition to Higher Grade education was an exciting experience, for Bellahouston Academy on Paisley Road (West) was, to an impressionable twelve year-old, an imposing building with a central tower and classrooms for the eighteen 1st, 2nd and 3rd year classes and seven Primary classes, with a large Assembly Hall, offices and staff rooms. Two outbuildings in keeping with the main building housed a gymnasium and swimming pool in one and four science labs., three Art rooms and classrooms for 4th, 5th and 6th year classes in the other. School uniform in navy blue and gold colour included a blazer with badge (a torch held aloft with the motto below — Alere flammam), navy blue short trousers, stockings with striped top and a navy blue school cap with stripes radiating from a top button. Girls wore navy gym tunic with gold blouse. Most pupils wore school uniform regularly, although the boys had discarded the school cap by third year and had also started to wear long trousers by that time. The blazer and the school tie (navy and gold stripes) continued to be worn until fifth and sixth year. All members of staff wore academic gowns, and the headmaster wore a mortar-board. The school day began with an Assembly of the whole school in the hall. In first year boys and girls were allocated to separate forms in ability ranges determined by performance in the "Qually". 1A, 1C and 1E were boys' classes; 1B, 1D, 1F were girls' classes, and this arrangement was maintained with very little variation throughout the first three years. A/B and C/D classes had French in addition to English, History, Geography, Maths, Science plus, of course, P.E., Art, R.E. E/F classes had no French. In second year A/B and C/D classes could add Latin or German to their group of studies. The school leaving age was one's fourteenth birthday and there was, after completion of second year a gradual whittling away of numbers especially in the E/F classes. Most A/B, C/D pupils stayed till the end of third year when a certificate

146

examination set by an external authority [The Day School Leaving Certificate (Higher)] was undertaken by all pupils, but certificates were presented only to those who left school.

At the fourth year stage, courses leading to the H.L.C. (Higher Leaving Certificate) began. So great had been the leaving rate at the third year stage that fourth year was organised as two classes A and B based on anticipation of presentation in 5th year on Higher or Lower Grades. There was no longer separation of boys and girls classes. It should be explained that the Higher Leaving Certificate was a group certificate — to gain the certificate it was necessary to pass in at least four subjects — two on the Higher Grade (of which one must be English) and two on the Lower Grade. A and B classes in fourth and fifth years were taught the same subjects at the same time so that a pupil might be in the A class for Higher French and the B class for Lower Maths. Another feature of the fourth year curriculum was the possibility of starting Latin, German, Greek for presentation on the Lower Grade in fifth year and Higher in sixth. It should be noted too that Higher English consisted of four papers — (1) Composition (2) Interpretation and Language (which included Vocabulary, Grammar, figures of speech, derivations, style etc.) (3) Literature (there were no set books, but a question on Shakespeare's plays was compulsory and the paper always included a question on Chaucer's Prologue to the Canterbury Tales and it was reasonably certain that there would be questions on the great English poets, dramatists and novelists) and (4) History (the first question, which was compulsory required short answers on ten important events or personalities chosen from a list of 15 to 20 — e.g. Galileo, Lister, death of Alexander III, marriage of James IV and Margaret Tudor etc.) The rest of the paper, if memory serves, was in three sections — Ancient, medieval, modern — and candidates were required to answer two questions. To gain a pass in Higher English it was necessary to pass in all four papers. Thus failure in the History paper meant failure in Higher English. One further feature of the H.L.C. examinations was that the written examination was supplemented by an oral examination conducted at a later date by H.M. Inspectors of Schools.

Social activities played a very big part in the life of Bellahouston Academy. The Dramatic society (membership fee one shilling) met regularly and presented a programme (usually of three one-act plays) each year. The Literary and Debating Society (membership fee one shilling) was open to pupils in third, fourth, fifth and sixth year and it met every Monday evening in the winter and spring terms. Meetings were very well-attended and inter-school debates and visits were held. Sports Clubs met for training on various evenings during the week. There were also choirs and music groups. As most of the school clubs organised a dance at the beginning of the season and one at the end pupils were well provided with entertainment. There was, of course, also a big Christmas dance. During the winter Glasgow Corporation arranged that pupils in 4th, 5th and 6th attend six Wednesday afternoon concerts given in St. Andrews Halls by the Scottish Orchestra conducted by Sir John Barbirolli. Bellahouston Academy also had a strong Former Pupils' club which took a keen interest in school activities and gave great support to school clubs.

University entrance did not have the complexities which seem to exist today. Application was made direct to the University chosen — there was no Universities Central Council on Admissions (U.C.C.A.) — and provided one's qualifications for the course to be followed were in order and the course approved by the Adviser of Studies, admission was granted. In the 1930s, no Government grants were available for students. Scottish students received a grant from the Carnegie Trust — for a degree course in the Faculty of Arts the amount of Carnegie grant was nine pounds per annum. After the war, a government Further Education and Training Scheme was introduced for returned service personnel, and this led on eventually to the introduction of grants for all students. Also for those whose studies had been interrupted by war service the period of training at Teacher Training College was reduced from one year to two ten-week terms. A five-week period of teaching practice under supervision in Glasgow schools was carried out in each of the ten-week terms. On completion of the training course I submitted applications for posts to Inverness County Council and to Aberdeenshire. I was appointed to the post of Assistant Teacher of English and History in Inverness Royal Academy and I took up duties there in April 1947.

Little had changed in school organisation or curriculum or the attitude to the teaching of English from the circumstances of the 1930s. Inverness Royal Academy was an academic establishment and most pupils who qualified for entry had the intention of staying on for Highers. Pupils were allocated to the Academy or to the Technical High School on the basis of "Qually" results. Both schools also had intakes from the surrounding countryside, from the West Coast and also from the outer islands — Harris, Skye, North and South Uist. The Higher examinations remained as they had been in the 1930s. Pupils wore school uniform, and prefects were distinguished by a gold trim round the edge of the blazer. Morning Assembly in the school hall was very formal and was quite impressive. In addition to the usual school clubs — Rugby, soccer, shinty, hockey, tennis, etc. — Inverness Royal Academy had an excellent Outdoor Club which made regular weekend trips to the Cairngorms, Glencoe, Ben Nevis, Wester Ross. Two fortnight-long summer holidays were spent in Glen Brittle in Skye when interesting climbs were undertaken in the Cuillins.

After the atmosphere of Inverness it was quite a change to visit Fortrose Academy on the first Saturday after notification of appointment to the post of Principal Teacher of English subjects to find the headmaster W.D. MacPhail M.A. (Hons. Classics), B.A. (Hons. History) clad in shorts and the kind of jersey favoured by Lewis fishermen, with a whistle on a cord round his neck and carrying his football boots on his way out to the King George V Playing field to referee a hockey match. Morning assembly to which pupils were summoned by hand bell on the first day of taking up duty (April 6th 1953) underlined the change of atmosphere, for the assembly was held in the old stone-floored canteen with its trestle tables and long forms and sounds of meal preparations in the background. This canteen was a detached building situated where the Deans Road entrance now is. Before long this same canteen was to be used as a classroom on some occasions, and enthusiasm for the beauties of Shakespeare's verse or the subtleties of Shavian wit could be considerably dampened by the off-stage sounds of plates, knives and forks being washed and, as it seemed, thrown with some force into receptacles. The canteen too served the further purpose of providing the venue for the staff morning tea-break (ten minutes). It was also the meeting-place for the Parent-teacher Association and, when suitably decorated, it served as the Christmas party dance-hall, stone floor notwithstanding. The school had no gymnasium. P.E. classes were held in what was at that time the Drill Hall (later MacKerchar Hall and now the Roman Catholic Church). There was no Technical Room, but Woodwork was taught in Charlie Mackenzie's workshop — the building between the Merrythought Cafe and the plumber's showroom. A second detached building on the Deans Road side nearer Academy Street housed the visiting Art teacher and his classes on two days of the week, and on two others it served as a Domestic Science room. School concerts, end-of-term prize-giving, H.L.C. exams and any other events of outstanding importance were held in the Town Hall.

In 1953 the school had a Primary Department of some one hundred pupils with the seven Primary classes taught in four classrooms by four teachers. The Secondary department staff consisted of five full-time teachers plus the Rector who taught all the Latin and some History, and six visiting teachers of Art, P.E., Woodwork, Domestic Science and Singing. The Secondary Roll was also about one hundred. The Rector taught his classes in Room 5 usually with the door open so that he could hear the office phone or see any visitor who arived at the school. Secretarial staff was employed on a part-time basis. Room 5 was situated roughly where the inner half of the dining hall now is i.e. from the dining hall edge of the stage to about the door into the kitchen. Room 4, the English classroom, extended from that door to the clock tower. The small space under the clock tower served as a library of a kind and a store-room for home-readers. From the windows of Room 4 and indeed of all rooms one had an uninterrupted view across the Firth and along the Moray coast. There were at that time no more than twelve houses between Deans Road and the lighthouse.

Avoch School and Cromarty school had Junior Secondary departments at that time, and the intake to Fortrose Academy included all Fortrose Primary pupils irrespective of promotion exam results and also those pupils from Drumsmittal, Tore, Avoch, Munlochy, Killen, Peddieston, Newhall and Cromarty who qualified for Senior Secondary education. There was also a very small intake from Avoch and Cromarty Junior Secondaries at the third year stage but it was considered necessary that they should repeat second year. Allocation to Senior Secondary was now decided by a Promotion Board, chaired by the Depute Director of Education along with two members of the Education Committee, three Primary headteachers, the Rectors or Deputies of Dingwall, Fortrose, Invergordon and Tain Academies and Plockton High School and the recently appointed County Psychologist. On the basis of the Promotion examination which had replaced the old qualifying exam and which consisted of attainment tests in English and Arithmetic supplemented now by two IQ Tests and a teacher's estimate mark and comment, pupils were placed in categories S1, S2, S3, J1, J2, J3. The Ross-shire Promotion Board was generous in its allocation to S (Senior Secondary) places and in addition J1 pupils were very often granted S placing. Appeals from parents backed by teachers' reports were dealt with at a follow-up meeting of the Board and again were treated with very careful consideration.

Pupils in first three years of Secondary school were allocated to A and B classes according to Promotion Board assessment, but A classes in Fortrose far outnumbered B classes as Junior Secondary pupils except those from Fortrose Academy had been allocated to Avoch and Cromarty. On many occasions, however, A and B pupils were combined as were 5th and 6th year pupils. By present day standards conditions seem difficult. There were no limitations on numbers in classes; non-teaching periods for teachers could be as few as three; and on occasions, as already mentioned, the canteen had to be used as a classroom. The staffroom too served sometimes as a classroom. The two staffrooms (one for men and one for women) which were both very small and were furnished with one table and about four upright chairs, the Rector's office and the boiler room occupied one side of the corridor in what is now the area between the two gymnasia. On the other side of the corridor were the Science laboratory and Primary classrooms. The construction of the extension which is now part of the woodwork room was under way in 1953 and was completed early in 1954. By 1960 staffing and accommodation were causing anxieties. A Latin teacher had been appointed and this released the Rector for administrative duties, but two teachers did not have classrooms and had to move from room to room throughout the day. Increase in the school roll and lack of a Gym and proper technical and Home Economics departments led the Rector to make representations to the Education department for increased accommodation. For a time nothing was done and the problem became more and more serious. A Parent-Teacher Association had been formed which, besides being a very real success socially, gave great support to the staff in applying pressure for new building. Eventually the Rector invited an influential local member of the County Council to present the prizes at the annual closing ceremony and, in his Rector's Report, he put the case for new building in the strongest possible terms. The Press reported his speech in full, and things began to move. Before long, plans were drawn up, staff were consulted about requirements, the County Architect addressed the Parent-Teacher Association, builders arrived on the site and the first phase of the new building was begun. This first phase consisted of the building of that part of the present school which projects from the front of the stage of the Assembly Hall to the Music and Home Economics rooms. Although great interest was taken in the progress of the building, the work was carried out with surprisingly little disturbance to classes, which continued as usual in the old building. On completion of Phase I a massive transfer operation was mounted in one day, and classes were established in the new rooms with a minimum of fuss. The transformation was astonishing. Classrooms equipped with excellent rotary blackboards, wall notice-board panels, wash basins, shelving, wall cupboards and walk-in cupboards in every room, along with a carpeted, curtained staffroom with comfortable modern furniture, tea and coffee-making facilities, a library with study room, purpose-built Home Economics, Science, Music accommodation, a well-equipped Rector's room and adjoining office all combined to make the new building a tremendous success with teachers and pupils alike — and that was only Phase I.

The Second phase provided the stage of the Assembly Hall, Technical Metalwork and Woodwork rooms, the Dining Hall and Kitchen, a gymnasium and Primary classrooms. This necessitated the provision of accommodation for Primary classes while the work was proceeding, and temporary classrooms were erected on the Deans Road side of the school. It was at this stage that some inconvenience arose for the natural curiosity of primary pupils led them to explore the nearby works area and, despite advice and warnings, shoes and sometimes clothing were spattered with mud. Parents complained and teachers were annoyed at the state of classroom floors. The rector suggested that pupils bring slippers for wear in classrooms but this was not altogether successful. However, the problem was short lived, and Phase two was soon completed and Primary classes were rehoused in classrooms extending from about the Deans Road entrance to the woodwork room. Between Primary 7 and the corridor beside the stage was a large General Purposes room which was to be used for talks to larger groups, meetings of groups such as Scripture Union, lunch-time debating and quiz meetings etc. It also housed the large Television set. The gym and changing rooms and the technical rooms extended from the rear of the stage to the Deans Road wall. The dining hall and kitchen premises occupied the remaining space towards the clock tower. It was felt that retention of some of the features of the old building had been most successfully incorporated in the creation of the new. When Phase two was complete the opening ceremony of the school was performed in the Assembly Hall at 3pm. on Monday, 23rd October, 1967, by Major Allan Cameron, Chairman of the Education Committee.

By this time, it should perhaps be noted, H.L.C. had become S.C.E. (Scottish Certificate of Education) and it was no longer a group certificate. Certificates were granted on the basis of passes in individual subjects. Teachers were no longer required to provide an estimate mark for pupils; instead an order of merit was required with a red line drawn to indicate division between expected pass and fail, and the visits of inspectors for oral examinations had been discontinued. S.C.E. examinations could now be held within the school. The Gym was used for that purpose.

It is interesting to recall that, when the County Architect Mr Leask, addressed the Parent-Teacher Association before building began, he pointed out that it was always the case that, between the drawing of plans for a new school and the actual occupation of the building by pupils, the school was already too small. Despite what seemed at first to be excellent provision of accommodation his words proved to be true at a fairly early stage and the shortage of accommodation was exacerbated by four factors which meant considerable change. The first of these was the closure of the Junior Secondary departments in Avoch and Cromarty and transfer of all Secondary pupils to Fortrose. This was to some extent compensated for by the transfer of all Fortrose Primary pupils to Avoch. The second factor was the introduction of the 'O' Grade certificate examination which was intended to encourage pupils to remain in school until the end of fourth year. The third was the raising of the school leaving age to sixteen (R.O.S.L.A.) which meant a greatly enlarged fourth year. House-building programmes too raised the school roll — especially at first at North Kessock and it was not very long before a new building was needed to house the Maths department, History, Geography and Art. By this time, of course, single-teacher departments were a thing of the past and the only visiting teachers were those who gave instrumental tuition in woodwind, brass, strings and piping. Alongside the development of established departments new departments were introduced e.g. Business Studies, Modern Studies and Navigation. The General Purposes Room was now required as a classroom and it was refitted to serve as the Business Studies Room and in fact had to be partitioned to form two rooms. With the development of North Sea oil and later with the opening of the Kessock Bridge, housing development in the Black Isle increased considerably and the Fortrose Academy catchment area was extended to include Culbokie. Further classrooms were required and demountable buildings were erected in the area east of the main building, and these housed History, Modern Studies and Science classes. A second gymnasium had been added earlier.

While building development was taking place, considerable changes were being made in curricula in teaching methods and in syllabus content in all subjects. To some extent the introduction of the 'O' Grade examinations was responsible. Mathematics was the first subject to undergo major changes, and teachers of other subjects began to examine methods and syllabi. A Central Committee on English was established and several week-long conferences were held to consider and formulate a new approach to the teaching of English. Local Development Centres were formed and met frequently. As a result many changes were made in the teaching of English and this was reflected in the type of question which appeared in 'O'-Grade and Higher English papers. Where most of the plans for change had been on a departmental basis during the 1970s, the late 1970s and early 1980s saw the workings of the Munn and Dunning committees which were concerned with curricular and assessment changes.

An early feature of school management that should be recorded was the Local Education Sub-Committee which functioned as a liaison between local schools and the Education Committee. This local committee also dealt with such matters as truancy, transport contracts, safety of pupils etc. Represented on the committee were the staffs of Primary schools, usually the head teacher, a representative from Fortrose Academy, the local council, the church and parents.

In 1955 the Academy had considerable involvement in the celebrations of the Quincentenary of the Royal Burgh. Various sports events were held, and the practice of 'beating the bounds' was begun. Four senior pupils from the Academy were started off by the Provost from the bridge at Rosemarkie, and they followed the line of the boundary of the Royal Burgh and reported to the Provost at a school concert in the Town Hall, Fortrose, in the evening. They each received from the Provost a commemorative medal. Also, at the time of the Quincentenary, the Burgh Council had had a new Coat of Arms prepared. It was thought that this could be used as a school badge and the Rector made enquiries in this connection. He was informed that the school could not use the burgh coat of arms but could use it with an academic difference as a school badge. The three volumes on a chief were added and the school badge was matriculated by the Lord Lyon King of Arms. At about this time the plaque containing the names of former rectors of the Academy was gifted to the school, and was unveiled in the front entrance of the old Academy by Mrs Cameron, daughter of former rector, Mr Laverie.

One other change in S.C.E. arrangement should be recorded. The 'O'-Grade examination was not a pass/fail examination. Certificates were presented on a 5-point scale A, B, C, D and E according to performance in the exam. A, B and C represented ranges over fifty per cent. Eventually this same system was introduced for results in the Higher examination. University entrance requirements were affected by this. Where before passes had been required, Universities now required A gradings in certain subjects.

During Mr MacPhail's rectorship the major changes that took place in the school were accommodation and staff changes. He looked for high academic standards and at the same time he encouraged sports, music, debating etc. although at that time it was difficult to maintain after-school activities because of transport problems. For a time pupils' bus passes (on public transport to Cromarty, Munlochy etc.) could be used on any bus, but the bus company decided to limit the use of the passes to the 4 p.m. bus. This made after-school sports, choirs etc. very difficult. This was an example of the kind of situation which exercised the Local Education Sub-Committee.

Mr Macleod inherited from Mr MacPhail a school that was very well-established academically and that had a considerable reputation for good results. In addition to academic qualifications Mr Macleod had business experience which he brought to bear on the running of the school. He felt that the establishment of a strong school fund was a priority, especially a fund which could allow the school to purchase and maintain a minibus of its own, and to this end he encouraged fund-raising activities — sponsored walk, annual sale with P.T.A. support, concerts etc. He recognised the educational value of modern equipment and Fortrose Academy became noted for its possession of T.V., video machines, photocopiers, duplicators, and the school led in the introduction of computers. Other innovations of Mr Macleod's leadership of the school were his development of a timetabling system which allowed for a weekly departmental meeting and for reasonable non-teaching time for all teachers. Each year the new timetable was prepared early enough to allow it to be operated from the beginning of June. This had two advantages. It meant that the month of June could be used as a start of the new year of work, and it also meant that problems could be ironed out in June and class work could start without any delays in August. He also introduced the practice of having a full week's visit of the incoming first year classes to accustom them to secondary school.

In the 1970s the Qualifying or Promotion examination had been discontinued and promotion to Secondary school was automatic. Head teachers received schedules from Primary Schools which showed I.Qs. and teachers' comments. The total roll of Fortrose Academy (Secondary Dept.) in 1953 had been about one hundred. In 1982, the year in which I retired, the intake to First Year was in excess of one hundred. Where in 1953 there had been one A class and a very small B class in first year, there were now in 1982 six first year form classes, each of approximately seventeen pupils grouped in four mixed ability classes following a common course. Although the intention was that classes should be organised as mixed ability groups for the first two years of Secondary school it was found necessary to make some adjustments and by the end of first year some streaming and some adjustment of the common course were made.

By 1982 the earliest changes envisaged in the Munn and Dunning reports were beginning. New courses were being planned and new methods of assessment were being proposed. This modern situation is for someone else to comment on.

The screech of the slate pencil on slate has given way to the clicking of the keyboard, and the whirr of the print-out. The major changes that have taken place nationally and locally have been attended by gains and losses. Fortrose Academy's building, staffing and curricular developments brought great gains in widening sporting and cultural horizons for the young people of the area. Sporting activities were extended to include journeys to Aviemore for ski-ing instruction, the introduction of Rugby football, cross-country running, netball and basketball, sailing and orienteering. School musical activity has developed from the singing lessons of the early 1950s to the introduction first of a recorder group and later to instruction in stringed instruments, brass and woodwind and piping which led eventually to the formation of an excellent school orchestra and to the very accomplished production of the musicals which have been so widely acclaimed. Curricular changes brought the gains of new subjects — Modern Studies, Navigation, Metalwork, Engineering, Business Studies etc. Great gains indeed! The losses may not seem to match these gains, and they may arise from personal feeling but they are worth a mention. In the 1950s with a full-time staff of about six and another six visiting teachers, all members of staff knew not only all the one hundred pupils but also all the parents, and there was about the school almost a family atmosphere in which the whole community shared. With increased numbers of pupils and staff and widening of the catchment area something of that atmosphere has been lost and it is to be regretted. Regrettable too has been the loss of Classics as an important feature of the curriculum.

Eheu fugaces labuntur anni!

Mr D. W. Macleod took this photograph of Mr Mackenzie and the senior pupils enjoying an outing to the west coast around 1960.

ACKNOWLEDGEMENTS

Thanks are due to a number of people for their help and for their permission to quote from newspaper articles and/or to use their photographs:

"INVERNESS COURIER"   IAN RHIND, CULBOKIE
"PEOPLE'S JOURNAL"   SKYVIEWS AND GENERAL LTD.
"PRESS AND JOURNAL"   H. TEMPEST LTD.
"ROSS-SHIRE JOURNAL"   G. WHYTE, INVERURIE
"THE NORTHERN CHRONICLE"

Class photographs of the 1920's have been used; they were taken by D and W PROPHET, of Dundee. Unfortunately, I have not been able to trace the company, whose representatives took school photographs for many years.

Thanks are extended to the Highland Region's Department of Architectural Services for permission to include copies of school plans.

A MOST SINCERE THANK YOU!

The production of this magazine would not have been possible without the support of many people, all of whom gave their help most willingly in a variety of ways. A number endured lengthy interviews most patiently and/or handed over photographs, giving permission for copies to be made. Some contributors wrote their own articles; several were approached — at moments which must have been most inconvenient — and asked to provide details of photographs or explanations of past events. Every single request for help was met with keen interest and practical support. A number of contributors have in addition provided useful suggestions for the investigation of other local History topics which are to be undertaken to meet the needs of new S.C.E. History courses.

This account has been compiled as a unit of work for use in Standard Grade History, and, as such, its length has had to be restricted to meet the time limits of the syllabus. It would require the preparation of many further editions to do justice to the History of Fortrose Academy on its present site — not to mention its History before 1890. In fact, some themes which had early been considered for inclusion have been omitted entirely.

Many thanks are due to those whose names are listed, in alphabetical order, on this page. It should be said that the list is not exhaustive.

Mrs C. Bassindale   Mr M. MacIver   Mr L. Murdoch
Mrs E. Brown   Mrs A. Mackay   Mr W. Noble
Mr C. Ferguson   Mr A.G. Mackenzie   Mr H. Patience
Miss A. Fraser   Mrs J.M. Mackenzie   Mrs K. Patience
Mrs M. Fraser   Mr D. Macleman   Mrs M. Sinclair
Mr A. Gow   Mrs J. Macleman   Mr A. Sutherland
Miss J. Hay   Mr D.W. Macleod   Mr D. Sutherland
Mr M. Kirkwood   Miss E. MacLeod   Mr E. Sutherland
Mr K. Lorraine   Mrs C. MacQueen   Mr J. Sutherland
Miss M. McCarrell   Mr R. Macrae   Mrs H. Wilson
Mr A. MacDonald   Mrs M. Moir   Miss H. Young
Mr F. MacIntyre   Mrs K. Munro

And our pupils   Craig Mackenzie
of the 1980's   Dianne Patience
                        Debbie Staines
                        The pupils of 2R and 3R